Hesitant Heroes

Aeneas and Turnus. Virgil, *Bucolica, Georgica, et Aeneis* (Paris: Didot, 1798).
Junius Spencer Morgan Collection of Virgil. Department of Rare Books
and Special Collections. Princeton University Library.
Courtesy of Princeton University Library.

Hesitant Heroes

Private Inhibition, Cultural Crisis

THEODORE ZIOLKOWSKI

Cornell University Press

Ithaca and London

First published 2004 by Cornell University Press

Printed in the United States of America

Library of Congress Cataloging-in-Publication Data
Ziolkowski, Theodore.
   Hesitant heroes : private inhibition, cultural crisis / Theodore
Ziolkowski.
      p. cm.
Includes bibliographical references and index.
   ISBN 0-8014-4203-6 (alk. paper)
   1. Heroes in literature.   2. Hesitation in literature.   I. Title.
   PN56.5.H45Z56 2004
   809'.93352—dc22   2003020657

Cornell University Press strives to use environmentally responsible
suppliers and materials to the fullest extent possible in the publishing
of its books. Such materials include vegetable-based, low-VOC inks
and acid-free papers that are recycled, totally chlorine-free, or partly
composed of nonwood fibers. For further information, visit our
website at www.cornellpress.cornell.edu.

Cloth printing   10 9 8 7 6 5 4 3 2 1

For Hans and Linda Reiss

Contents

Preface

The hesitant hero first caught my attention many years ago. Writing *Virgil and the Moderns* (1993), I became aware of the intense debate among classicists surrounding Aeneas's moment of hesitation in the concluding verses of the *Aeneid*. But the different set of questions that concerned me in that book, which dealt with the reception of Virgil in the twentieth century, prevented me from pursuing the matter. Later, as I was studying Aeschylus's *Oresteia* in connection with *The Mirror of Justice* (1997), I was struck by the wavering of Orestes in *The Libation Bearers* just before he carries out his vengeance killing of Clytemnestra. Again, my primary concern at the time with the legal issues in the third play of the trilogy, the *Eumenides*, distracted me from thinking through the implications of that sublime moment in the middle play. But the similarity between the two cases, so wholly at odds with the customary image of the hero, continued to tease at my imagination and alerted me to analogous examples in other literary works with which I had been long familiar. This book is the result of my continuing efforts to understand those exceptional cases and their larger implications.

This book also represents my homage to the teachers who introduced me to many of the works discussed here. I first read Virgil while I was in high school. Since my school in Montevallo, Alabama, offered no Latin, my parents arranged for me to take private lessons for several years with Edgar C. Reinke of what was then called Alabama College for Women. It was with that fine classicist, after football practice on autumn afternoons in 1947, that I first read the *Aeneid*. While I was an undergraduate at Duke University, several outstanding teachers fostered my literary interests (and converted me from pre-medical studies to the humanities). There I read parts of *Wallenstein* for the first time with Clement Vollmer and parsed out my first Greek tragedies in the classroom of James N. Truesdale. While I had read *Hamlet* in school, my indoctrination in the serious study of Shakespeare came at Duke in Alan Gilbert's seminar. During a subsequent Fulbright year in Innsbruck I attended a seminar on the *Oresteia* offered by Robert Muth. My fascination with *Parzival*, and with the medieval world generally, was fostered during evening *privatissima* in his New Haven apartment by my *Doktorvater* Hermann J. Weigand while I was a graduate student at Yale; and Weigand's Schiller seminar profoundly deepened my understanding of *Wallenstein*. Following those memorable days and evenings more than fifty years ago I had the opportunity to teach several of these masterpieces in various courses at Princeton and to write about most of them, albeit in other contexts, in various books and articles. Certainly those texts have never been far from my mind, and each rereading reminds me of my debt of gratitude to teachers whose learning and love of literature offered an inspiring model for me.

All translations, unless otherwise indicated, are my own; for reasons of critical precision I have sought to translate as literally as possible. The editions cited are specified in the notes; for the reader's convenience I have used widely available standard editions.

It is not only to past mentors that I owe my gratitude. I began writing this book while spending the autumn of 2001 in Berlin, thanks to the generosity of a Humboldt Senior Research Prize. For sharing with me their helpful books on Virgil I am indebted to Michael C. J. Putnam of Brown University and Richard F. Thomas of Harvard University. I am grateful for the opportunities that I enjoyed in the spring of 2002 to share my ideas on the "hesitant hero" with two wholly different groups. The Sunday Evening Seminar at Christ

Church, Christiana Hundred, near Wilmington, Delaware, offered the opportunity to formulate my thoughts in a manner accessible and plausible to a widely varied audience of intelligent and interested nonspecialists. The participants in the Graduate Research Workshop on the Classical Tradition at Harvard University challenged me to deal with texts and contexts in a manner acceptable to knowledgeable specialists in various cultural periods. Cornell University Press found the ideal reader for my manuscript in Susan Ford Wiltshire, a distinguished classicist and comparatist, whose insights helped me to sharpen my argument at several crucial points. Bernhard Kendler shepherded the manuscript through the editorial process with gratifying enthusiasm and incisive suggestions. It is a pleasure to acknowledge the editorial acuity and congenial sense of style that Jane Dieckmann brought to my manuscript. As usual, for their interest, encouragement, contributions, and responses I am indebted to my family research center: Gretchen the Slavicist, Jan the medievalist, and Eric the scholar of religion. My wife Yetta— who also studied Latin with Edgar Reinke, pondered *Hamlet* as an undergraduate English major in Montevallo, read the Greek tragedies and medieval epics as a graduate student in Comparative Literature at the University of North Carolina in Chapel Hill, and shared my affection and respect for Hermann Weigand—has long been my most challenging *Gesprächspartnerin*. She joins me in the expression of warm friendship over many years conveyed in the dedication.

THEODORE ZIOLKOWSKI

Princeton, New Jersey

Hesitant Heroes

Introduction: The Paradox of the Hesitant Hero

Epic heroes do not hesitate in the thick of action. Achilles may sulk at first in his tent, but when he sallies forth to battle he triumphs in a cold rage over Hector and then drags the body mercilessly around the walls of Troy before the appalled eyes of the slain warrior's father and mother. Odysseus lingers for ten years in various Mediterranean ports, but when he finally reaches home he dispatches the suitors and lynches Penelope's shameless serving women without batting an eye. Beowulf eagerly seeks out an occasion to battle the ogre Grendel and then plunges boldly into the foul mere in pursuit of the monster's fiercer mother. Hildebrand, returning from exile (in the Old High German *Lay of Hildebrand*), unflinchingly kills his son in single combat in order to redeem his own honor. The biblical heroes are no less impulsive, though to be sure they are sustained by the conviction that they have a higher power on their side. "In the name of the Lord of hosts" the shepherd boy David, who has confronted lions and bears fearlessly, dashes quickly forward with his sling to attack the giant Goliath and then straightway beheads the stunned Philistine (1 Sam. 17.41 ff.). When "the Spirit of the Lord came mightily upon him" (Judg. 14.5 ff. and 15.14 ff.) Samson tore the young lion asunder and smote one thousand Philistines with the jawbone of an ass. The message is unmistakable: we expect heroes to act without hesitation.

Why, then, do some of the most famous heroes of literature pause at crucial points of the plot in the very heat of action? At his moment of triumph over Turnus, which marks the end of his epic tribulations, Aeneas restrains his hand and hesitates for a few moments before plunging his sword into the enemy's breast. At the central turning point of the *Oresteia* trilogy Orestes, who has returned to Mycenae in order to avenge his father's murder, vacillates for precious minutes before he drags Clytemnestra away to the slaughter. Parzival, arriving at the Castle of the Holy Grail, in the face of his obvious suffering neglects to ask the fateful question that will heal the Fisher King and thereby delays the prophesied process of redemption for more than four years. Hamlet, having convinced himself of Claudius's guilt in the murder of his father and catching the king at an unguarded moment, puts away his sword and postpones his revenge to a more appropriate time. And in Schiller's dramatic trilogy *Wallenstein,* the hero, once the victoriously decisive general of the Thirty Years' War, delays and temporizes over his allegiance to the emperor until it is too late to save his career and his life. What do these hesitations tell us about the nature of heroism? about the relationship of the hero to his world? about the writer's view of his or her own society?

In each case the text contains plausible psychological motivations for the hero's hesitation. Aeneas is momentarily swayed by the youthfulness, abject surrender, and pleas of Turnus. Orestes is temporarily taken aback when confronted with the harsh realization that the murderer he must kill is his own mother. Parzival, still a naïve bumpkin at that early point in the epic romance, falls back on superficial rules of courtly etiquette rather than following the impulses of his heart. Hamlet persuades himself that he should not kill his uncle at prayer lest the murderer's soul be spared the eternal damnation that it deserves. Wallenstein, wishing to keep all his options open to the last possible moment, waits until he is certain that the most favorable astrological conjunction has occurred—tactical delays that culminate in an evening of hesitation with fatal consequences. All these works, epic and dramatic alike, display a profound and subtle understanding of the human psyche.

But these masterpieces contain implications that reach well beyond the personal psychology of their heroes. When I began to analyze the paradox more systematically, the word "inhibition" presented itself as the proper technical term. Roger Smith's informative study *Inhibition* helped me to understand the history and meaning of the term in the fields of neurophysiology and psychology and to appreciate the varied causes underlying inhibitions and hesitations. His concluding suggestion that "readers without a specialist interest in the history of science . . . might wish that it [his book] had pursued inhibition into literature or into the political economy of society" encouraged me to think further about the implications of the subject in literature.[1] Freud's ruminations in *Civilization and Its Discontents* (1930) led me to the insight that the moments of private hesitation—that is, inhibited or repressed action—that had caught my attention could also signify, in great works of literature, turning points in cultural history, epochs of conflict between value systems, and ultimately the collapse of those systems, long before the post-Cold-War "clash of civilizations" identified by Samuel P. Huntington in his widely debated book of that title (1994). Civilization, Freud argues (see Chapter 1 below), progresses by repressing basic erotic and aggressive tendencies inherent in humankind. But at moments of great excitement or stress the cultural restraints give way and allow the ancient instincts to surface again with destructive violence—a pattern that seems with well-nigh schematic accuracy to explain Aeneas's behavior vis-à-vis Turnus.

In the light of Freud's theory, I suggest, the hesitant heroes can further be seen as exemplifying crises in the cultures that have brought them forth. The momentarily inhibited actions of Aeneas and Orestes expose, though in wholly different ways, a deep-lying conflict between the ancient culture of blood vengeance from which they are emerging and the future civilizations of law and justice that they envision. Parzival's failure to ask the symbolic question stems from a tension between the instincts of the religious culture in which his mother has raised him and the courtly society to which he has been superficially exposed. Hamlet's vacillations are catalyzed by the apparition of his father's ghost, an intrusion of the irrational into his rationally ordered world which challenges and indeed shatters the habits of mind in which he has been schooled, leaving him intellectually defenseless before the demands suddenly made upon his emotions. And Wallenstein is caught in a web of conflicting polarities claiming his loyalty—the Holy Roman Empire and the invading Swedes, Catholicism and Protestantism, calculation and superstition. In each case, in other words, the hero's hesitation or inhibition reflects crises inherent in the greater world he exemplifies.

These cultural crises, implicit or explicit within the texts, reflect in turn stresses that the poets sense within their own societies. The emotional tensions momentarily paralyzing Aeneas and Orestes foreshadow the potential political violence that Virgil and Aeschylus perceived as underlying the still fragile civil societies of Augustan Rome and of Athens in the decades following the Persian Wars. Wolfram von Eschenbach took up the Celtic myth of Parzival as a mirror in which to reflect the struggle between church and state, between emperor and pope, which was raging in early thirteenth-century Germany. The old Germanic legend of Hamlet provided Shakespeare with a vehicle for analyzing the epistemological anxieties of contemporary England in which the philosophical skepticism of the Renaissance was undermining the sustaining beliefs and binary thought patterns inherited from the Middle Ages. And Schiller, writing in the 1790s, saw in Wallenstein an exemplary case of the individual caught between freedom and necessity, a theme that obsessed the poets and thinkers of German idealism, while the Thirty Years' War provided an ominous foreboding of the wars threatening Europe in the Revolutionary Age.

The classic hero so fully accepts and so perfectly embodies the values of his culture that he experiences no doubts or hesitations: the archaic blood vengeance motivating Achilles, the Germanic code of honor driving Hildebrand, the religious faith sustaining David. Hegel maintained (see Chapter 6 below) that such classic heroes emerged from the same cultures that created epic or other narrative genres as the form providing the ideal vehicle for the expression of heroic virtue. As the classic forms were transformed in the face of industrialization, urbanization, commercialization, and other alienating forces of the modern world, so too the hero in his original purity and immediacy of action had to change. The "hesitant" hero can be viewed as an early symptom of this vast social transformation: an epigone, a man so born so late that he is torn between opposing systems of belief and value and becomes incapable of the same unthinking action that characterized his heroic predecessors.

This sequence, of course, displays degrees of variation. For Aeneas and Orestes, in whom the veneer of civilization barely laminates the old vengeance culture, the hesitation is a matter of moments. In Parzival the brief minutes of inhibition cause a delay of more than four years—a period during which he matures to the point at which he can embrace and reconcile oppositions that are already firmly rooted in his world. Hamlet's moment of vacillation is preceded by two months of doubts and delays, and his tragic hesitation ultimately bears a tremendous cost in bloodshed, which even then results in no lasting reconciliation of forces. Wallenstein, finally, temporizes so long that his delays render him fatally incapable of action in a complex world of multiple conflicts. In sum, we observe a progressive intensification as the hero passes from instant action through momentary hesitation to ever-lengthening delays and temporizations culminating in total inaction. This development, which parallels the growing complexities and religious-political-epistemological conflicts of Western civilization, is accompanied by a shift from narrative epic to drama, as the genre in which the psychological motivation of the hero can be more profoundly analyzed, and eventually to the novel, as the focus shifts from the inaction of the hero to the pressures of the world surrounding him.

What happens to the hero who has passed through these various stages? He reaches the state of permanent vacillation or wavering that was observed and analyzed by Sir Walter Scott in the figure whom he ironically introduces as "our hero" and who bears the telling name "Waverley." Waverley, the Englishman who can never make up his mind between North and South, between Scotland and England, Catholic and Protestant, ancient community and modern society, manages—unlike Wallenstein, who is destroyed by his inability to act—to resolve his conflicts by marrying a Scotswoman and settling down on the border between the two countries and cultures. From Waverley it is an easy step to the "passive heroes" of Dickens and Thackeray and to those neurotically introspective "sick heroes" and self-obsessed "antiheroes" who populate French and Russian literature of the nineteenth century with their indecision and inaction—Julian Sorel and Frédéric Moreau, Dostoyevsky's nameless Underground Man and Pechorin, whom Lermontov sardonically labeled "a hero of our own times." (It is revealing that the term "hero" began to be commonly, and often ironically, applied to the central figure of fictional works about the time that it began to lose the force of its original cultural meaning.)

When writers of the nineteenth century wanted to confront their (almost inevitably hesitant) heroes with heroic dilemmas, they had to send them, like Conrad's Lord Jim, away from the West into exotic lands where conflicts between cultures were still taking place or, like Melville's Billy Budd, into the self-contained communities of ocean vessels where a naive sense of justice and honor by its very existence challenges the established order. Failing such exile, these figures end up in the multicultured and multivalued twentieth century like the "hero" of Unamuno's novel *Mist,* so uncertain in the face of choices and unable on his doorstep to decide whether to go left or right that he simply waits until he can fall in behind a passing dog; Franz Kafka's Josef K., who spends the last year of his life postponing and ultimately rejecting the decision to accept responsibility for his guilt; or T. S. Eliot's Prufrock, who has "time yet for a hundred indecisions."

This book does not aspire to set up a typology of heroes in the manner of such works as Joseph Campbell's *Hero with a Thousand Faces* and C. M. Bowra's *Heroic Poetry* or to categorize "traditional types" after the model of Gilbert Murray's *Hamlet and Orestes*.[2] Instead, it seeks through the analysis of examples to ascertain the shifting meaning of the terms "hero" and "the heroic." Focusing on the hero as a mirror of his age, it suggests how larger cultural crises are exposed through the moments of hesitation experienced by literary heroes as they metamorphose from the hero as apotheosis of his culture to the Romantic hero as alienated individual. Private hesitation, in other words, constitutes the fissure through which we enter the public world of these often quite different fictions. The crises of those fictional worlds anticipate, finally, the tensions that the writers sense in their own contemporary reality. Through the psychological and social analysis of hesitant heroes, in sum, this book seeks to contribute not only to our understanding of specific literary texts but also to the cultural history of the epochs portrayed in them and of the periods that brought them forth.

Obviously, I am making no attempt after the fashion of an old-fashioned *Stoffgeschichte* to catalog here all the examples of hesitation in world literature which might occur to other readers. The works that most readily suggested themselves to me, given my education and interests, are universal poems of the sort designated in German as *Weltgedichte*. Together they exemplify significant stages in the history of Western civilization: from Greek and Roman antiquity by way of the Christian Middle Ages and Renaissance down to the modernity of the nineteenth and twentieth centuries. Furthermore, as I suggested in the opening paragraph, these examples stand out because they differ so sharply from many classic works featuring utterly dissimilar types of heroes. This book aspires, rather, to provide representative models of analysis, interpretation, and contextualization which may be applied to other literary works as well as the cultural backgrounds that they depict and in which they were composed. It would be fascinating, for instance, to learn from an Indologist to what extent our Western examples are consistent with culture and motivation in the *Bhagavad-Gita*. The great Hindu epic is premised on the hesitation of the warrior Arjuna, who—unlike the Germanic Hildebrand—throws down his arms at the thought of killing his kinsmen in the opposing army. Krishna succeeds through the complex theological arguments for which the work is famous in persuading him to take up his arms and engage in his ultimately victorious battle.[3]

And what about heroines? one might reasonably ask at this point. It is conspicuous, at least in literary history, that the women rarely hesitate. Clytemnestra, Elektra, and Antigone, Salome, Judith, and St. Joan: whether they intend to slay their husbands or to behead

John the Baptist and Nebuchadnezzar's general, to honor their brothers or incite them to murder their mothers or to liberate France from the English—all of them act unflinchingly and with conviction, often motivated by a religious faith as mighty as their swords. While it would be worthwhile to pursue the topic in other contexts—the exciting 1995 exhibition in the Kunstmuseum Düsseldorf entitled "Die Galerie der Starken Frauen" ("Gallery of Strong Women") for example—the *hesitant* heroine would appear on the surface to be a contradiction in terms.

It is no rhetorical *captatio benevolentiae* but simple common sense if as a comparatist I grant at the outset that I am not trying to compete with the specialists on their own ground. As my notes indicate, I have drawn gratefully on the work of classicists, medievalists, Renaissance scholars, and modernists in my effort to understand the specific texts with which I have dealt. Max Weber maintained in his lecture "Scholarship as a Calling" (1919) that studies reaching over into neighboring disciplines ought to be undertaken "with the resigned awareness that one can at most offer the specialist useful questions which might not so readily occur to him from his specialized viewpoint, but that one's own work must inevitably remain highly incomplete."[4] But Weber, as his magisterial works amply demonstrate, was too modest. What the comparatist has to offer is the comparative overview, the surprising conjunction of works infrequently brought together, and the reciprocal illumination of similarities and differences alike which is achieved in the process. That is the aim of this project on the fascinating and illuminating paradox of the hesitant hero. And if, as I propose in the conclusion, this approach to literature and its heroes enables us to understand something about our own times (the receiving culture), that insight will be an additional benefit.

1

Aeneas, or Hesitation in Hesperia

THE CONTEXT

The concluding lines of Virgil's *Aeneid* have aroused more con-
tention and controversy than any ending in the history of European
epic.[1] Everyone who studied Latin in school or attended a Great
Books course in college will remember the circumstances. Following the fall of Troy and pursued by the fury of a wrathful and
unforgiving Juno—"saevae memorem Iunonis ob iram" (1.4)—Aeneas leads his fleet of Trojans around the eastern Mediterranean
for seven years in search of the promised new homeland in Hespe-
ria (Italy). Fleeing plague and drought, attacked by foul Harpies,
enduring violent storms at sea, and lamenting the death of his father Anchises, he arrives at last on the coast of Africa, where Queen
Dido is building her glorious new city. Succumbing for several
months to a passion for the Tyrian queen, Aeneas is at length ad-
monished by Jupiter's messenger Mercury to leave the fleshpots of
Carthage and continue on his destined path. After a brief sojourn
in Sicily he arrives on the coast of Italy and is accompanied by the
Cumaean Sibyl on a visit to the nether world, where he encounters
the shades of lost companions as well as the embittered Dido, who
took her life following his departure. There, too, the shade of his

9

father Anchises reassures him with a vision of the future history of Rome, featuring a pageant of heroes culminating in Virgil's own patron, Augustus.

Following these eight years of wandering (bks. 1–6, Virgil's response to Homer's *Odyssey*), the events of the second half of the epic—corresponding to the *Iliad*—move much more rapidly (taking less than a month's time). Fortified by his father's prophecies but also warned by the Sibyl that he must endure terrible wars— "bella, horrida bella" (6.86)—before achieving his goal, Aeneas continues along the coast of Italy to the mouth of the Tiber, where he is welcomed by Latinus, king of Latium. Latinus's daughter, Lavinia, is wooed by many suitors, but the king has been warned by an oracle not to wed his daughter to any native suitor and to await the arrival of an outsider. Taking Aeneas to be the destined husband and successor from abroad, the king pledges him his daughter's hand—an action that offends the queen, who has long favored the most attractive and powerful of the local princes, the Rutulian Turnus. Incited at Juno's behest by the Fury Allecto, Turnus stirs the native Italian tribes to war against the Trojan interlopers. Aeneas goes off to seek allies among the Etruscans and, in particular, among the Arcadians, whose king Evander has founded a city on the future site of Rome. While Aeneas is gathering confederates, Turnus and his forces attack and almost overwhelm the Trojan camp on the seacoast. Hastening back with his new allies, Aeneas wards off the attackers but, in the process, suffers the loss of Pallas, Evander's son, whom the Arcadian king had entrusted to his care. Arranging a truce with the Latins, Aeneas agrees to settle the issue through single combat with Turnus. Again, however, war breaks out and many warriors on both sides are killed—including the Italian warrior maiden Camilla—before the duel finally takes place.

First hurling their spears, they close in for hand-to-hand combat. Aeneas is still limping from an arrow wound, but when Turnus's swordblade shatters, Aeneas pursues him five times around the battleground. At length Turnus's sister, the goddess Iuturna, hands her brother another sword, and Aeneas recovers his spear from the roots of an olive tree. As Aeneas prepares to charge, Turnus picks up a huge stone—larger than twelve normal men could lift—and hurls it at his enemy. The stone falls short and Turnus, deserted by his sister (who has been called off by the gods) as well as by his strength and courage, trembles at the sight of Aeneas's mighty spear. Awaiting his moment, Aeneas hurls his weapon, which pierces Turnus's thigh, forcing him to his knees while the hills and groves resound with the groans of the Rutulians. As Aeneas towers over him, Turnus acknowledges his defeat before the assembled armies and the surrender of the Italian tribes to the Trojans. He concedes Lavinia to Aeneas as his future wife and urges Aeneas not to carry his hatred further ("ulterius ne tende odiis," 12.938). Moved by this appeal, Aeneas hesitates:

> stetit acer in armis
> Aeneas, volvens oculos, dextramque repressit;
> et iam iamque magis cunctantem flectere sermo
> coeperat.
>
> (12.939–41)

(Fierce in his arms, Aeneas stood still, casting his eyes about, and restrained his hand; and gradually the words began to sway him as he hesitated.)

At this fateful moment he catches sight of the sword-belt that Turnus had torn from the corpse of Pallas and now wears as a sign of his own triumphs. This sight, this "token of cruel grief" ("saevi monumenta doloris," 12.945), rekindles Aeneas's fury and wrath ("furiis accensus et ira / terribilis," 12.945–46). Crying that he will not allow Turnus to escape his vengeance and that in Pallas's stead he demands atonement from Turnus's impious blood, Aeneas buries the sword in his enemy's chest. The scene, and the entire epic, ends with the laconic verse—already familiar to the reader because it has been used once before to characterize Camilla's death (11.831):

> vitaque cum gemitu fugit indignata sub umbras.

(With a groan his soul, aggrieved, fled to the shades below.)

THE PROBLEMATIC ENDING

Attention has long been focused on the ending in part because it is so abrupt, lacking any "diminuendo and healing threnody."[2] Rather than opening out into the future, as is the case in most epics, it leads our thoughts down into the underworld with the dejected soul of the defeated Turnus and leaves us there. (Aeneas's own descent into the underworld in book 6 ended, by contrast, with his ascent back through the ivory gate into the world above.) In the *Iliad,* which provided Virgil's specific model for the last six books, Hector's death at the hands of Achilles takes place almost two thousand lines before the end.[3] It is followed by an elaborate description of the funeral games played by the Greek heroes in honor of Patroclus (bk. 23) and by the circumstances leading to the dignified burial of Hector by the Trojans (bk. 24). The duel between Achilles and Hector, while the highpoint of the epic, thus recedes into a larger context. Similarly, at the end of the *Odyssey,* after Odysseus has slain the suitors, Athena descends from heaven to arrange a covenant of peace between the warring groups. And, at the other end of the epic spectrum, the archangel Michael sends Adam and Eve out of Eden on "their solitary way" (*Paradise Lost,* 12.649) into the brave new world, but only after having consoled Adam with an extensive vision of paradise regained.

Its very abruptness, then, has led readers for generations, indeed centuries, to pay special attention to the ending, in which "two voices" were recognized long before Adam Parry's now classic essay.[4] The early commentators, to be sure, were not troubled by Aeneas's deed. Such Christian exegetes as the sixth-century monk Fulgentius, whose *Virgiliana Continentia* was widely read in the Middle Ages, regarded the *Aeneid* as an allegorical account of human life, beginning with the shipwreck, which represents the birth through which man enters the storms of life. All the figures Aeneas encounters have an allegorical function in his life. The episode with Dido suggests the passion of youth, while marriage to Lavinia represents a life of labor and achievement. The duel with Turnus symbolizes his triumph over anger (*furibundus sensus*) and obstinacy (Iuturna) and the ultimate victory of wisdom.[5]

The secular writers of the high Middle Ages, though they sacrificed allegory for contemporary relevance, were equally untroubled by the ending. In Heinrich von Veldeke's late twelfth-century epic *Eneide* (based on the anonymous Old French *Roman d'Eneas*) Aeneas's duel with Turnus, elaborately portrayed in terms of a knightly tournament, is simply an important incident in the second of two episodes of courtly love and is almost an anticlimax following Lavinia's extensive reflections on *minne*. (Aeneas chops off Turnus's head when he notices that Turnus is wearing the ring that Aeneas had earlier given to Pallas.) The hero must overcome his passion for the experienced beauty Dido before winning the hand and kingdom of the lovely maiden Lavinia. After Turnus's death the poem goes on for another thousand lines, providing an extended description of the wedding feast, whose splendor can be matched, the poet assures us, only by the festivities that Emperor Friedrich Barbarossa arranged in Mainz (1184) to celebrate the investiture of his two sons.[6]

The sense that the epic ended too abruptly and without a suitable conclusion inspired other poets, from the fifteenth century down to the late nineteenth, to compose a thirteenth (and even a fourteenth) book to complete Virgil's *Aeneid*.[7] The most successful and famous among these was Mapheus Vegius's *Libri XII Aeneidos Supplementum*, which first appeared in manuscript in 1428. Following its publication in 1471 it regularly accompanied most editions of the *Aeneid* published in Europe and Britain for the next two centuries and inspired commentaries, translations into the major languages, and a series of six woodcut illustrations by Sebastian Brant.[8] Vegius also reduces the slaying of Turnus to a transient moment and shifts the reader's attention immediately back to Aeneas.

> Turnus ut extremo devictus Marte profudit
> Effugientem animam, medioque sub agmine victor
> Magnanimus stetit Aeneas, Mavortius hero . . .
>
> (1–3)[9]

(When Turnus, conquered in his final battle, poured out his fleeting soul, great-hearted Aeneas stood victorious between the armies . . .)

The poet then recounts how Aeneas, sitting on Turnus's corpse, accepts the surrender of the Rutulians. After retrieving Pallas's sword-belt, he sends Turnus's body to his father Daunus for a proper burial (in imitation, of course, of Achilles, who returns Hector's body to Priam). Shortly thereafter Aeneas's marriage to Lavinia is celebrated, and Aeneas builds a new city named for his wife. Succeeding Latinus, Aeneas rules for three years and then dies, cleansed of his mortal remains in the waters of the river Numicius and translated in spirit by his divine mother Venus into the heavens, to be honored henceforth by the Julian line as their family deity.

> Tum Venus aerias descendit lapsa per auras,
> Laurentumque petit: vicina Numicius undis
> Flumineis ubi currit in aequora harundine tectus.
> Tunc corpus nati abluere, et deferre sub undas
> Quicquid erat mortale iubet: dehinc laeta recentem,
> Felicemque animam secum super aera duxit:
> Immisitque Aeneam astris, quem Iulia proles
> Indigetem appellat, templisque imponit honores.
>
> (623–30)[10]

(Then Venus descends through the airy skies and seeks out Laurentum, where Numicius, shaded by reeds, flows in rivery waves to the nearby sea. Then she orders that the body of her son be washed clean and that whatever was mortal be carried away by the waters. From there, joyous, she conducted his fresh happy spirit with her into the heavens where she inserted Aeneas among the stars—Aeneas, whom the Julian clan calls its founder and honors in its temples.)

During the later Renaissance the ending began to claim the attention of sixteenth-century critics who applied to it the contemporary code of honor based on Aristotle's *Nicomachean Ethics*.[11] In book 3 of Antonio Possevino's *Dialog dell'honore* one disputant argues that Aeneas loses our respect at the end because it is dishonorable to kill one's opponent. He can justify Virgil only by assuming that, had he lived, he would have changed the ending. Perplexed by this conflict between the canonical epic and contemporary theories of honor, Torquato Tasso and other poets offered variations on the contest between Aeneas and Turnus as examples for the de-

bate over chivalric courtesy versus Virgilian dishonor. In canto 7 of
Gerusalemme liberata the single combat between the Christian knight
Raimondo (substituting for Tancredi) and the pagan warrior Argante is interrupted when Argante's sword breaks (as does Turnus's). When Raimondo hesitates over the two options—that is, to
spare his enemy's life or to kill him—Argante attacks again and almost wins the fight, which ends indecisively. In canto 19 the duel is
resumed with Tancredi now again facing Argante. When at length
Argante is wounded, Tancredi offers him the chance to surrender.
Because Argante repeatedly refuses and tries to stab his opponent,
Tancredi is finally forced to kill him as a last resort. Again, however,
the Virgilian solution is toned down by the continuation of the romance with a final canto, in which the captain of the Christian
knights, Goffredo, spares his wounded pagan opponent Altamoro.
The dilemma that occupied the minds of Virgil's Renaissance admirers,[12] however, largely disappeared during the next three centuries.[13]

The late twentieth-century controversy between the "two voices"
or the positive and negative readings of the *Aeneid* did not begin, as
is sometimes assumed, as a product of the 1960s and the Vietnam
protests. As early as 1951 Robert Lowell, himself a conscientious ob-
jector during World War II, published his poem "Falling Asleep over
the Aeneid."[14] The epigraph sets the scene, a Sunday morning in
the spring of 1945: "An old man in Concord forgets to go to morning service. He falls asleep, while reading Vergil, and dreams that
he is Aeneas at the funeral of Pallas, an Italian prince" (*Aen.* 11.29–
99). Although the poem eschews all editorial comment, Lowell has
chosen a passage that enables him, by re-creating and partly trans-
lating Virgil's lines, to examine his own ambivalent attitude toward
wars—their horror as well as their tragic necessity—ranging from
Aeneas's wars against the Italian tribes and the second Punic War
down to the American Revolutionary War, the Civil War, and World
War II. Lowell's attitude represented a striking departure from the
tone set by most other Anglo-American poets of the 1930s and
1940s. In the United States such writers as Alan Tate, Donald Davidson, and John Peale Bishop almost ritually summoned up Virgil's
world as an ideal against which to measure the present and viewed

the *Aeneid* as an analogue for a Europe plunging again into war.[15] In England, T. S. Eliot—both in his poems and in several essays— reflected the attitude that led, in 1943, to the founding of a Virgil Society with the aim of demonstrating Virgil's relevance to the problems of the modern world and of exposing the *Aeneid* as a testament to "civilized consciousness and conscience."[16] On the Continent, meanwhile, Theodor Haecker's widely translated tribute *Vergil. Vater des Abendlands* (*Virgil: Father of the West,* 1931)[17] anticipated on a popular level the tone of the leading German classicists, who after a long period of neglect were rediscovering Virgil as a representative of Augustan *humanitas.*[18]

It was against this trend that certain classicists in the United States and Britain began to oppose a darker view of the *Aeneid.* Kenneth Quinn's summation, in his subtly nuanced psychological reading of the scene, is typical.

> We must condemn the sudden rage that causes Aeneas to kill Turnus when he is on the point of sparing him—and when his death no longer makes sense, for Turnus has acknowledged defeat (936–7); the war is over and the peace terms already agreed to (187–94). The killing of Turnus cannot be justified, this is beyond doubt the judgment expected of us.[19]

By 1976, W. R. Johnson was able to state that one could discern "two quite distinct schools of Vergilian criticism that seek to explain and to justify the *Aeneid* by constructing for it two radically opposed political allegories."[20] The more optimistic European school saw in the *Aeneid* the "triumph of virtue over unreason" and the vision of "a transcendental cosmic order."[21] The so-called Harvard school, in contrast, questioned the grandeur of Augustan Rome and detected in the *Aeneid,* instead of affirmation, "the beginning of the age of anxiety" and Virgil's recognition that Rome along with Aeneas is caught in the power of darkness. That the debate, which has enlivened classical studies of recent decades, goes on today is evidenced by such scholars as Richard F. Thomas, who argues that "Augustan" readers from antiquity to the present have routinely suppressed the ambivalence and anxiety underlying Virgil's work.[22]

I propose to shift the emphasis slightly—away from the actual act of killing to the moment of hesitation that immediately precedes it. The scene has not gone unremarked, of course. One of Virgil's earliest commentators, the late fourth-century grammarian Servius, devoted several lines to the exegesis of Aeneas's hesitation: "[The poet's] whole intention is devoted to the glorification of Aeneas: for because he contemplates sparing his enemy, he is shown to be pious; and because he slays him, he carries out an act of piety: out of consideration for Evander he avenges the death of Pallas."[23] More recently, one classicist has observed that it constitutes "an extraordinary moment of humanity; for the epic warrior never hesitates."[24] Another, in a thoughtful and incisive chapter devoted to that very moment, concludes that it "does speak out to humanity more movingly" than the more visionary passages of the poem.[25] Yet a third has suggested that Aeneas's hesitation "shows the reality of the possibility" that his vengeance "might not have needed to happen."[26] Accordingly a leading German Virgil scholar has remarked that the concluding scene of the *Aeneid* is the key to the entire work.[27]

TO KILL OR NOT TO KILL

Psychologically, Virgil has provided us with a plethora of cues by which to explain Aeneas's fury and wrath. Not only has Pallas been entrusted to Aeneas's moral and military tutelage by his father Evander; during their brief acquaintance they become closely bonded—notably during the overnight boat voyage (10.159–62) from the city of the Etruscans back to the besieged Trojan encampment. While "great Aeneas" ponders the issues of war, young Pallas sits at his side and inquires about the navigational significance of the stars and about Aeneas's own adventures on land and sea. Following Pallas's death the next day in glorious but unequal combat with Turnus, Aeneas grieves at length, contemplating his unfulfilled pledge to Evander and the loss of Pallas's support in the future establishment of Rome. He covers the youth's corpse with a robe of gold and purple woven for him by Dido and sacrifices captive Latins in his honor, sprinkling the flames with their blood (11.29–99). All this crosses his mind as he stands over the kneeling

Turnus and recognizes Pallas's sword-belt. And indeed, the narrator had prophesied earlier, when Turnus tore the belt from Pallas's body, that he would live to regret that rash act.

> Turno tempus erit, magno cum optaverit emptum
> intactum Pallanta, et cum spolia ista diemque
> oderit.
>
> (10.503–5)

(The time will come when Turnus will have paid anything to have Pallas unharmed and when he will hate those spoils and that day.)

But the belt with its "familiar plaques" ("notis . . . bullis," 12.942) involves an additional motive. For as we know from an earlier description (10.497–99) the plaques are embossed with the story of a notorious crime ("impressumque nefas"): the cruel slaying of a band of youths by their brides on their wedding night ("una sub nocte iugali / caesa manus iuvenum foede"). Virgil feels no need to recount the entire story of the fifty Danaids, who—with one exception—slew the fifty sons of their uncle Aegyptus, to whom they had been forceably married, because his readers would have provided the necessary details from their own cultural knowledge. In any case, it is not merely a familiar belt that Aeneas sees across Turnus's shoulder, but a belt which through its mythological subject encourages him to his bloody act of vengeance. Hence, as has been suggested, Aeneas's hesitation involves not only indecision but recollection.[28] Memory ties Aeneas to the dark past as powerfully as vision pulls him toward the bright future. There are other factors as well.

After all, Turnus is responsible in a very specific sense for all the slaughter than has taken place in two pitched battles. He shattered the peace and instigated the war by breaking treaties not just once, but—at least indirectly—twice. The first time, driven into a fury by Allecto and "raging with the love of the sword and the impious frenzy of war" ("saevit amor ferri et scelerata insania belli," 7.461), he incites his Rutulians to march against Latinus and to defend Italy against the Trojans. The second time, after he has agreed to meet Aeneas in single combat, the Rutulians are whipped up by his deified sister Iuturna, who has assumed human guise, to join Turnus in his battle against the Trojans. If he is spared, what is to prevent him—say, after the death of the much older Aeneas—from attacking Aeneas's son Ascanius and, retroactively, undermining Aeneas's dreams of empire?

Turnus has been portrayed as animal-like in his ferocity and violence. He prowls around the Trojan battlements like a wolf around a sheepfold (9.59–66), snatches a fleeing combatant from the walls like an eagle seizing a hare (9.563–64), and rages in the Trojan camp "like an enormous tiger among the slothful herds" (9.730). Later he kills two brothers and hangs their heads, dripping with gore, from his chariot (12.511–12).[29] There is even a hint that, as a European, he is afflicted by a certain racist hatred, or at least contempt, of the "Asian" invaders from Troy. (Virgil clearly sees the conflict between the Trojans and the native Italians as one between the two worlds of Europe and Asia: "quibus actus uterque / Europae atque Asiae fatis concurrerit orbis," 7. 223–24; and "quae causa fuit, consurgere in arma / Europamque Asiamque," 10.90–91).[30] Turnus rails against the "deserter from Asia" ("desertorem Asiae," 12.15) and scoffs at his enemy's effeminate Phrygian garb and hair curled with heated irons and soaked in perfume ("loricamque . . . semiviri Phrygis et . . . crinis vibratos calido ferro murraque madentis," 12.98–100). All these aspects appear to confirm Spengler's view that the battle of Actium unleashed the fears of an ancient civilization grown antiquated vis-à-vis an Arabic culture on the point of emerging.[31]

Despite his youth and beauty, however, despite our sense that he is somehow an innocent victim of the wiles of Juno and Allecto, despite the affection of his sister, despite his growing awareness that he has been deserted by Fate and the gods, Turnus is destined to die. Aeneas in one sense becomes little more than the instrument of that death. Still Aeneas hesitates. Why? Turnus has appealed to his sense of parental grief.

> miseri te si qua parentis
> tangere cura potest, oro (fuit et tibi talis
> Anchises genitor), Dauni miserere senectae

> et me, seu corpus spoliatum lumine mavis,
> redde meis.
>
> (12.932–36)

(If any concern for an unhappy parent can touch you, I pray [for Anchises was such a father to you], take pity on Daunus's old age and return me—or, if you prefer, my body deprived of life—to my kinsmen.)

No matter that Turnus was deaf to all such appeals himself and exulted over the death of the overmatched young Pallas, placing his foot on the corpse and telling the Arcadians to bear word to Evander that he is returning his son to him "in the condition he deserves" ("qualem meruit, Pallanta remitto," 10.492). Nevertheless, Aeneas, having recently lost his own father and keenly aware of his responsibility to his own young son, is affected by a sense of parental sympathy.

When Aeneas encounters his father's shade in the underworld, Anchises advises him to disaccustom his heart from warfare and to cast from his hand his weapons ("ne tanta animis adsuescite bella . . . proice tela manu," 6.832–35). In perhaps the most famous passage of the entire poem his father's shade goes on to instruct him that it is the destiny of Rome not to cultivate the arts and sciences but, rather, to rule over nations, to impose peace, and—with a vivid dialectical contrast of *sub* and *super*—to spare the humbled and crush the haughty in war.

> tu regere imperio populos, Romane, memento
> (hae tibi erunt artes) pacique imponere morem,
> parcere subiectis et debellare superbos.
>
> (6.851–53)

(Remember, Roman, to rule the nations with your might—these are your arts—and to impose the custom of peace [or: to add civilized manners to peace], to spare the humbled and overcome the proud.)

Indeed, in his initial promise and prophecy to Venus regarding Aeneas, Jupiter assures her that her son will found a race whose destiny it will be to soften harsh ages and bring wars to an end ("aspera tum positis mitescent saecula bellis," 1.291) and to lay down laws. Later, when he sends Mercury to hasten Aeneas on his way from Carthage, Jupiter reiterates the mission of Aeneas's progeny to rule over an Italy teeming with war and pregnant with clashing tribes ("gravidam imperiis belloque frementem / Italiam regeret," 4.229–30) and to subject the entire world to his laws ("totum sub leges mitteret orbem," 4.231). In other words, Aeneas's moment of hesitation reflects among other things a tension between the inchoate lust for blood vengeance and the keen and clear sense of mission— to be firm but generous, humane, and lawful in his treatment of those he has subdued.

Finally, just as the contest between Turnus and Pallas was an unequal one between the experienced warrior and the young prince, so too all the onlookers are aware of the advantage held by the mighty Aeneas against the handsome young Turnus, whose youth is repeatedly emphasized, as is that of the warrior maiden Camilla. It is fitting, therefore, that the same resonant verse is used to characterize the death of both young warriors ("vitaque cum gemitu fugit indignata sub umbras"), in which the problematical vocable *indignata*—indignant, resentful, aggrieved—presumably encompasses the feelings of those deprived too soon of their lives. In any case, our sympathy—and Aeneas's—must be raised by the annihilation of youth.[32] So he hesitates.

Other key moments of hesitation are not unknown in the *Aeneid*.[33] We can safely ignore the "hesitation" of such inanimate objects as the wooden horse, which gets stuck four times at the gates of Troy ("quater ipso in limine portae / substitit," 2.242–43), or the golden bough that resists Aeneas's eager tug ("avidusque refringit / cunctantem," 6.210–11). It has been persuasively argued, however, that Dido's tarrying in her room before she emerges for the hunting expedition with Aeneas ("reginam thalamo cunctantem," 4.133) suggests her premonition of the grief to follow: her "marriage" to Aeneas when the storm drives them into a cave, his eventual desertion, and her suicide.[34] Later the shade of Anchises advises his son that he might have more to gain if he would occasionally hesitate like Q. Fabius Maximus, who won the nickname *Cunctator* from the delaying tactics by which he defeated Hannibal and restored the state: "tu Maximus ille es, / unus qui nobis cunctando restituis rem" (6.845–46). Turnus hesitates and is rendered speechless when Allecto first reveals herself to him in her most hideous form ("cunctantem et quaerentem dicere plura," 7.449). Even Vulcan hesitates as Venus beguiles him into making arms for Aeneas (8.388).

In their final confrontation, at length, we see both Turnus and Aeneas hesitate. When Turnus first realizes that he has been deserted by the gods as well as his own strength, he hesitates in fear ("cunctaturque metu," 12.916). Aeneas brandishes his spear and awaits the most auspicious moment to hurl it at his hesitating enemy ("cunctanti," 12.919). So it is almost with a sense of expectation and fulfillment that we come upon the final momentous hesitation as Aeneas listens to the pleas of the fallen Turnus and is momentarily swayed, for all the reasons cited above, by his words ("et iam iamque magis cunctantem flectere sermo / coeperat"). In the uncertain world of the *Aeneid* everyone experiences moments of hesitation—gods, kings, queens, and heroes. But are there larger implications?

INHIBITION: THE PAUSE THAT REPRESSES

The word "inhibition" has been used for centuries in law and theology to express prohibition, and notably to designate the imposition of political order and civilized values at the social level.[35] In the course of the nineteenth century and in accord with the manner in which order and disorder were regulated at the social level, it gained currency as a technical term in physiology and psychology—to designate how the mind or will regulates the body and how the brain controls physiological functions. By analogy, nineteenth-century writers were fond of comparing hierarchical government in human society to hierarchical control in the nervous system. In the early twentieth century, three major scientific schools emerging from earlier physiology focused on inhibition as a conceptual tool. Britain, and the English-speaking world generally, emphasized a purely scientific and microphenomenal approach, as exemplified by the neurophysiology of C. S. Sherrington, who explained events as the transmission of impulses along neurons and across synapses. In Soviet Russia, I. P. Pavlov applied Marxist theory to neurophysiology in an effort to interpret excitation, inhibition, and equilibrium in the brain as a dialectical process.

Like Sherrington and Pavlov, Sigmund Freud also emerged from nineteenth-century neurophysiology, which understood physiology as an expression of hierarchical control and inhibition. While the term "inhibition" (*Hemmung*) occurs frequently in Freud's writings, it never became an organizing concept as it did for his two contemporaries. Yet because Freud, especially in his later writings, tended to move from the specific to the general, from technical discussions to their larger social implications, it was principally his work that introduced the public to the idea that inhibition is both a product and a condition of civilized existence.

Freud's writings on cultural theory are pervaded by the theme that all civilization is based on the repression of natural instincts. As early as 1908 he argued that "every individual has renounced a piece of his possession, his total power, the aggressive and vindictive inclinations of his personality."[36] In that early study of "'Civilized' Sexual Morality and Modern Nervous Illness" Freud was concerned principally with the repression of human sexual instincts. A few years later, in "Timely Observations on War and Death," he insisted that "our culture has been achieved by renouncing the satisfaction of drives, and it demands of each newly arriving member that he accomplish the same renunciation of drives."[37] In this piece, written during the early years of World War I, Freud shifted his focus to human aggression, which needed to be suppressed in the interest of society and culture. A characteristic of these repressed drives, whether sexual or aggressive, is their "constant readiness at any suitable opportunity to break through to satisfaction" (145). War provides such an opportunity. "It strips away the later layers of culture and permits the primitive man within us to reappear" (160)—a primitive man, according to Freud, driven by the killer instinct. "The very emphasis on the commandment 'Thou shalt not kill' forces us to recall that we are descended from infinitely long generations of murderers, in whose very blood, as perhaps still in ours, the lust for murder coursed" (157).

In his masterful essay of 1930, *Civilization and Its Discontents*, Freud summarized his earlier thoughts, defining the two basic drives—sexual and aggressive—as Eros and Thanatos, libido and the death drive (the impulse to destroy).[38] Beginning with the now familiar assumption that the primordial and instinctive tendency to aggression represents the greatest obstacle to all civilization, Freud devotes the last two sections to an analysis of the means that civilization (*Kultur*) employs in an effort to hinder aggression, to render it harmless, perhaps even to invalidate it altogether. In this connection he stresses his conviction that the cultural process of humankind and the developmental process of the individual are similar in nature, and perhaps even the same process applied to different objects. The question of man's fate, he concluded in 1930, depends on whether and to what extent the human race will succeed in mastering the disruption of social and civic life through the human drive toward aggression and self-destruction.[39]

If, accepting Freud's analogy between the cultural process and individual human development, we regard the *Aeneid*, in one important sense, as the story of a civilization's development in its movement from Troy by way of Carthage to Rome, then Freud's observations provide a suggestive paradigm. (Although Freud knew Virgil well and used a quotation from the seventh book of the *Aeneid* as the epigraph for his early masterpiece, *The Interpretation of Dreams*, he does not cite Virgil's work in his studies of cultural theory.) First, Aeneas clearly had to repress Eros, his libido, when he chose to leave Dido in order to establish the new homeland in Rome. Once that initial civilizing step was accomplished, the second and, according to Virgil, more important step ("maius opus moveo," 7.45) still remained: to control his basic aggressive instinct—to become, as it has been expressed, "a hero in an age no longer heroic."[40] This need is implied in the words through which Anchises, during their conversation in the underworld (bk. 6), outlines the future course of Roman history and the principles by which Rome shall govern, and specifically in his admonition: "parcere subiectis et debellare superbos." In light of these precepts, as we have seen, Aeneas's duty vis-à-vis Turnus is clear: to spare him in defeat, now that his arrogance has been overcome. That is the behest of a civilization that has succeeded in repressing its destructive instincts toward aggression.

Freud, in his preface to the second edition of *The Interpretation of Dreams*, confessed that his work was "a piece of my self-analysis, as my reaction to my father's death, that is, to the most significant event in the life of a man."[41] By analogy, one might conclude that Aeneas's journey to the underworld and the insights into his mission provided there by his father represent, psychologically, his own reaction to Anchises' death a year earlier. (Freud, as we know from the epigraph to *The Interpretation of Dreams*, regarded Virgil's Acheron as the realm of repressed thoughts.)[42] Indeed, it might well be argued that only with his father's death does Aeneas begin to free himself from his Trojan past and to prepare for the Roman future.[43] In any case, we can readily agree that the motivation of Aeneas's act is much more complex than he himself consciously realized.[44]

But two circumstances interfere with the process of repression through civilization. First, as Freud noted, war strips away the superficial layers of civilization and permits the primitive instincts to resurface in all their violence: blood vengeance overcomes law. And, as we already know from many earlier passages (e.g., his behavior during the Greek sacking of Troy), Aeneas is susceptible to irrational ("amens," 2.314) bursts of fury and rage ("furor iraque," 2.316). Second, Aeneas stands at the beginning of the civilizing process of Roman history: he is still close to his Trojan roots; the habit of civil behavior is still only a hope, a project. Accordingly, we can see in his fateful hesitation—and we should not imagine it as lasting more than a few seconds—a manifestation of the tension between past and future, between the aggressiveness of primitive (pre-Trojan and non-Western) man and the civilizing tendencies of the Hesperian Roman *civitas* yet to come. Indeed, the "Gefühlsambivalenz"[45] that Freud defines as the characteristic of this hesitation is close to that "ambivalent" attitude that has been proposed as the proper balance between the "optimistic" and "pessimistic" inter-

pretations of the *Aeneid*.[46] That Virgil allows primitive aggressiveness to win out in the final lines of his epic suggests his awareness
of the long road that will lead from those early and still primitive
hero-kings to the *res publica* in which Anchises' idealizing vision will
be at least partially realized. *Kultur*, civilization, is not easily achieved
and must be constantly guarded and protected against the instincts
of terror and violence that never lie far beneath the surface.

THE HISTORICAL ANALOGY

That being said, what led Virgil to end his work—and I am writing
with the assumption that he consciously ended his masterpiece in
this way and did not simply leave it unfinished when he died—with
an act that has perplexed commentators from Servius to the present? Virgil (70–19 B.C.E.) came to maturity during a period of crisis, the great social revolution that marked the transition from the
late Republic to the early Principate. The turmoil of those decades—"a century of anarchy, culminating in twenty years of civil
war and military tyranny"[47]—exposed, with a violence rarely
matched in other periods of history, the sempiternal conflict between power and law. (It was their concern about the latest eruption
of this perennial conflict that in 1932 triggered the correspondence
on war between Freud and Albert Einstein.)[48]

In Roman history the conflict was precipitated toward the end of
the second century B.C.E. when the brothers Gracchi as *tribuni plebis*
through a series of legislative initiatives successfully sought to wrest
concessions for the people from the oligarchical nobility of the Senate. Following the death of the Gracchi, Sulla escalated this contest
between populists and optimates to bloody new heights. After his
victory in 82 B.C.E. over the populist armies, Sulla embarked on a
frenzy of vengeance that outdid anything in the earlier history of
the Republic, slaughtering everyone who had been associated with,
or even suspected of associating with, the populists.[49] He issued a
list of *hostes publici*—public enemies or "proscribed persons"—who
could be killed on sight. And he persecuted his enemies even beyond their deaths by means of the *lex Cornelia*, which specified that

the properties of proscribed persons should be auctioned off, that their sons and grandsons should lose the right to hold office, and that their slaves should be set free and become Sulla's own political "clients." In many senses Sulla's "reforms" in favor of the nobility amounted to a dictatorship that can be regarded as a precursor of the subsequent principate.

Sulla's dictatorship occurred in the decade immediately preceding Virgil's birth in 70 B.C.E. As a boy in Mantua, however, and as a student in Cremona and Milan, Virgil might well have heard his father and his teachers discussing the most recent manifestation of the contest—the notorious conspiracy of L. Sergius Catilina, which was immortalized in Cicero's four great orations *In Catilinam* (63 B.C.E.) and by Sallust's classic monograph, *De conjuratione Catilinae* (written some twenty years later). Here the roles are reversed. The consul Cicero, in his orations, emerges as the defender of law and order, that is, of the Senate, in opposition to the conspirator Catilina, who in his boundless craving for political power set himself up as an advocate of the people, the army, the non-Roman tributaries. Of particular relevance in the present context is Cicero's moral reasoning in his first oration, as he deliberates the question whether Catalina, now that evidence of the conspiracy has been betrayed in the autumn of 63 B.C.E., should be executed or simply exiled from Rome. While he would feel safer in the knowledge that his archenemy is dead—Cicero repeatedly reminds his listeners of the personal danger to which he continues to be exposed—it nonetheless seems to him prudent, even at the risk of being considered lax in his duties, to spare Catilina's life, lest anyone think that he had imagined or even concocted the entire conspiracy for political reasons of his own. In this famous first oration, which Virgil no doubt studied as a rhetorical model, the poet would have recognized a prolonged and explicit moment of moral hesitation of the sort that Aeneas fleetingly and implicitly experienced: to kill or to spare the enemy.

In the event, the point soon became moot. Catilina fled from Rome, and over the following weeks the evidence of the conspiracy mounted and became incontrovertible. In the debates that followed (and to which Cicero contributed the third and fourth of his orations), the Senate vacillated. Following a passionate appeal for the death penalty by consul-designate D. Junius Silenus, the members were swayed in the other direction by Julius Caesar, who typically recommended the milder sentence of life imprisonment for Catilina. After Cicero (in his fourth oration) called for a rapid decision, Cato in his capacity as *tribunus plebis* demanded the death penalty in a powerful speech that carried the day and the vote.

In Sallust's account of the conspiracy (notably sections 53 and 54), Caesar and Cato stand out as the two emblematic heroes—"ingenti virtute, divorsis moribus viri duo"—embodying different sets of virtues. While alike in family background, age, and eloquence, their spiritual grandeur ("magnitudo animi") manifested itself in different ways. Caesar was known for his generosity and munificence, Cato for his unblemished life ("integritate vitae"). The one was famous for gentleness and mercifulness ("mansuetudine et misericordia"), the other for moral rigor ("severitas"). Caesar achieved fame for his beneficence, Cato for his thrift. Caesar was praised for his friendliness ("facilitas"), Cato for his constancy ("constantia"). In sum: "in altero miseris perfugium erat, in altero malis pernicies" ("in the one, the unfortunate found their refuge; in the other, the evil their destruction"). Sallust's perceptive characterization recapitulates precisely the respective thrusts of their speeches regarding the fate of Catilina, who was killed in battle the following year along with his entire army. At the same time, it also reflects on a sublime level the two aspects of the Roman character exposed in Aeneas's deliberations: Caesarian clemency versus Catonian rigor.

Virgil was familiar, then, with widely known examples of violence versus law running through recent Roman history (as in the politically different cases of Sulla and Catilina) and of the deliberation between mercy and retribution (in the mind of Cicero and in the debate between Caesar and Cato). In a celebrated passage of the *Aeneid* (8.668–70) he contrasts the wholly different situations of Catalina and Cato in the underworld:

> et te, Catilina, minaci
> pendentem scopulo Furiarumque ora trementem;
> secretosque pios, his dantem iura Catonem.

(and you, Catalina, clinging to a threatening cliff and trembling at
the countenance of the Furies; and, set apart, the pious ones and Cato
giving them laws.)

Those tensions, he surely recognized, constituted a central theme
in the history of the *res publica.* But Virgil did not need to look only
to history, for he could directly witness similar tensions in the political personage to whom he was closest: Augustus.

It has been increasingly recognized by scholars that Virgil's epic,
as a historical allegory, must also be read as a commentary on his own
times.[50] During the years when Virgil was writing his epic (c. 29–19
B.C.E.), Augustus was in the process of accumulating and consoli-
dating that vast and assorted bundle of offices, powers, and *auctori-
tas* that we now, for the sake of convenience, designate as his
"principate" (even though the Romans had no single word to designate his position, and the term "caesar" had not yet been transformed from a family name into a political term).[51]

In his early *Eclogues,* to be sure, Virgil pronounced now famous
words of praise for the godlike ruler—still known as Octavian—
who had spared his family's farm from the lands seized to compen-
sate the victorious soldiers in the battle at Philippi in 42 B.C.E..

> O Meliboee, deus nobis haec otia fecit.
> namque erit ille mihi semper deus, illius aram
> saepe tener nostris ab ovilibus imbuet agnus.
> (Ecl. 1.6–8)

(O Meliboeus, a god has provided us with this leisure. For he shall always be a god to me; often a tender lamb from our folds shall stain his
altar.)

The *Georgics* also feature passages of praise, notably the description
of the temple that Virgil proposes to set up in Mantua in honor of
Augustus and on whose tapestries and doors will be depicted the
scenes of his deeds (3.16–39). Augustus is glorified in three key
passages of the *Aeneid* as well. In the great prophecy at the start of
the epic, where Jupiter assures Venus that her son Aeneas shall ultimately build his new city in Italy, Aeneas's family line is traced

down to Augustus, the "Trojan Caesar" (1.286), whose empire will
be limited only by the seas, whose glory will rise to the stars, and
who will close the grim gates of war. Again, when Aeneas encounters his father in the underworld, Anchises catalogs the succession
of heroes who will descend from Aeneas and his Italic wife, Lavinia,
a list culminating in the man often promised:

> Augustus Caesar, Divi genus, aurea condet
> saecula qui rursus Latio regnata per arva
> Saturno quondam, super et Garamantas et Indos
> proferet imperium.
>
> (6.792–95)

(Augustus Caesar, of divine descent, who shall again establish a
Golden Age in the fields once ruled by Saturn, and shall extend his
empire beyond the Africans and Indians.)

Finally, on the great shield that Vulcan crafts for Aeneas and on
which are depicted key scenes from the history of Rome, the deeds
of Augustus are featured (8.678–728), and notably the defeat of
Anthony and Cleopatra in the battle of Actium and the triple triumph with which Octavian was celebrated in 29 B.C.E.. By means of
these three prophetic passages Aeneas is subtly transfigured into a
prefiguration of Augustus himself.[52] Indeed, many contemporaries
may well have thought, as they listened to Virgil's account of the battle between Aeneas and Turnus, of the more recent conflict between Octavian and Antony.[53] One authority has even suggested
that it was the main purpose of the *Aeneid* to commemorate Octavian's victory in the battle of Actium.[54]

While such glorification of the emperor and acknowledgment of
the official ideology was expected and almost routine in poetry of
the principate, however, we are also aware of another darker, more
personal, and more critical tone.[55] Even as he was celebrating Octavian in his *Eclogues,* Virgil could hardly have been unaware of the
anger smoldering in most of the populace, whose properties had
not been excluded from the ruthless expropriations in the territo-
ries of some eighteen cities across the whole of Italy. The opening
Eclogue juxtaposes the contentment of the shepherd Tityrus with the

misfortunes of the disappropriated exile Meliboeus. In their thirst for vengeance against Caesar's murderers, Anthony and Octavian —who now presented himself as *divi filius* even though he was only the nephew and adoptive son of the assassinated Caesar—matched Sulla in their vindictiveness and showed little of that Julian *clementia* praised by Sallust.[56] They outlawed their political enemies, including some three hundred senators, established rewards for their deaths or capture, and auctioned off their estates. The proscriptions decimated the senatorial families and caused a radical realignment of political interests. After the battle at Philippi—and in close analogy to Virgil's portrayal of the Italian tribal warriors—Octavian sent Brutus's head to Rome for display. When these actions produced an anti-Octavian coalition of the dispossessed, which was concentrated in Perugia, Octavian was merciless in his reaction. On the anniversary of Caesar's assassination he executed some three hundred citizens of that city, including senators and knights, before an altar set up in honor of the deified Julius. In short, on the way from Octavian, adoptive son of Julius Caesar, to Augustus, from *dux* to *princeps*—political senator and consul, military *imperator,* religious *pontifex maximus,* honorary *pater patriae,* to mention only a few of his titles—Augustus provided many examples not only of the political astuteness, military prowess, and moral rectitude for which he was subsequently praised, but also of the cruelty, ruthlessness, and vindictiveness that according to Tacitus (*Annals* 1.9–10) began to be acknowledged publicly on the very day of his burial. (In our own time, a similar view informs Ronald Syme's memorable portrait in *The Roman Revolution,* written against the background of Europe in the 1930s, of Augustus as an implicit predecessor of twentieth-century totalitarian dictators.)

In sum, the moment of hesitation when Aeneas is torn between the claims of law and mercy and the lust for vengeance and death manifests not only the general tension produced, according to Freud, by the repressive forces of civilization over libido and aggressiveness—a tension that snaps when Aeneas glimpses Pallas's belt on Turnus's shoulder. It also exemplifies more specifically Virgil's understanding of the history of Rome during his own lifetime.[57] The

Aeneas who exacts vengeance for the death of Pallas prefigures in a very precise manner the *pietas* of Octavian, who avenged his adoptive father, Julius Caesar, by sending Brutus's head to Rome. Toynbee pointed to Virgil's awareness, as early as the dark ending of the first *Georgic,* of the growing schism in the Roman soul, its sense of drift and acknowledgment of sin[58]—a schism that Augustus sought to counter by imposing his revival of the ancient state religion. Virgil's acute awareness of the conflicting impulses in the Roman character—prefigured in the deliberations of Cicero, acted out by Caesar and Cato, and embodied by the contradictory actions of Augustus himself—may have prompted him by means of a subtle and indirect example to urge ("warn" is no doubt too strong a word) Augustus and his Roman audience to guard against that native bloodlust in the still uncertain and perilous years of the early principate. Some have persuasively argued that even in the prophetic passages of the *Aeneid* Virgil expresses a sense of ambivalence regarding Rome under Augustus.[59] Others have suggested that it was his failure to reconcile the two voices, to justify the dark side of the Roman character—and not aesthetic concern about incomplete verses— that caused Virgil on his deathbed to demand that the *Aeneid* be destroyed;[60] or, conversely, that he deliberately left it incomplete as an image of incompletion in Roman life and history.[61] But it might as well be argued that Virgil fully intended for his readers to confront the dilemma for themselves—that he "invited an ethical reaction"[62]—for he could easily have avoided the entire problem by permitting Aeneas to kill Turnus with the initial cast of his great spear.[63] After all, Virgil had invited us once before to consider Aeneas's ambivalence in a similarly dramatic scene. In the duel with Mezentius (bk. 10) Aeneas first wounds his enemy from a distance with his spear and then rushes in for the kill with his sword. Mezentius's son Lausus, however, intercedes to protect his father and then challenges Aeneas, who tries vainly to warn off the untested youth. If Aeneas realizes by the end that, for all his *pietas,* he is subject to the dark forces of the human condition, then the same applies mutatis mutandis or even a fortiori to Virgil and his times. The poem that set out to depict the origins of Rome gradually, in the course of its twelve years of composition, came to reflect on the author's own present and the nature of history itself.[64]

The *Aeneid* can thus be regarded in an important sense as the bildungsroman of a man destined to forsake myth for history, memory for reality, revenge for clemency, *furor* for *pietas*—"to leave the Trojan world of heroic and impetuous daring and inaugurate the Roman world of forethought, duty, responsibility (*pietas*)."[65] But, as is proved by the final irruption of irrationality, he grows not toward moral perfection but toward a more interesting and revealing human complexity and fallibility. When Aeneas hesitates over the wounded body of Turnus, he is torn between the blood vengeance of the old heroic world and the *humanitas* of a new civilized society—a world in which there is no place for the animal energy and barbaric violence of a Turnus. Yet it is surely an oversimplification to state that Turnus is "simply one of the casualties of civilization."[66] The tragic paradox of this epic moving toward psychological romance is that Aeneas must revert momentarily to that barbaric violence in order to free the world from its claims in the future. In an ironic inversion Turnus appeals with the voice of reason (his *sermo*) to an Aeneas who here reacts with fury ("furiis accensus")—a response that foreshadows Lucan's sobering conclusion in his *Pharsalia* several generations later that power and virtue seldom go hand in hand ("virtus et summa potestas non coeunt," 8.494–95).

This state of tragic ambivalence seems to be confirmed if we turn to an earlier work that deals with those same years immediately following the Trojan War, when the lessons of civilization were still too fresh, too superficial, to contain the repressed forces of violence and vengeance and whose hero exemplifies precisely the same tensions as those that beset Aeneas. The moment of hesitation, we begin to understand, often symbolizes an instance when the clash of cultures is manifested with devastating force in the psyche and actions of a single individual.[67]

2

Orestes, or Anguish in Argos

Pity poor Pylades! His role offers precious little scope for the aspiring actor. In the three classical dramas that depict the tragic action culminating in Orestes' murder of his mother Clytemnestra and her lover Aegisthus, he is scarcely more than a silent bystander and henchman. Condemned to an inglorious wordlessness in the *Electra* dramas of Sophocles and Euripides, he utters only three lines in Aeschylus's *The Libation Bearers*—the central play in the *Oresteia* trilogy.[1] But those lines, coming at a crucial point late in the drama, serve dramatically to highlight the significance of the moment. Let us set the scene.

THE CURSE OF THE ATRIDES

The series of murders ending with Orestes' matricide can be traced back to Orestes' great-grandfather Pelops, the son of Tantalus. (Tantalus himself had earlier offended the gods by attempting to serve them his son's flesh at a banquet; his famous punishment condemned him to eternal existence neck high in a pool of water that receded when he tried to drink and beneath fruit trees whose branches remained always just out of reach.) As a suitor seeking to win the hand of Hippodamia, the daughter of King Oenomaus, Pelops is challenged to outrace her father. He wins by bribing the king's charioteer to remove the linchpin of Oenomaus's chariot. But rather than rewarding his co-conspirator, he hurls him into the sea.

The curse thus called down upon his house, and involving a succession of seductions and family murders, continues through the next three generations, beginning with Pelops's sons, Atreus and Thyestes. Because Thyestes seduces his brother's wife, Atreus banishes him from his kingdom. Later, under the pretext of reconciliation, he invites Thyestes back to Mycenae, where in revenge he serves him a stew featuring the flesh of Thyestes' own sons. Thyestes, cursing the house of Atreus, flees and subsequently has another son, Aegisthus, by his own daughter, Pelopia. Meanwhile Atreus's sons, Agamemnon and Menelaus, marry the sisters Clytemnestra and Helen. After Helen is seduced by Paris and carried off to Troy, Agamemnon leads the Greek armies against the Asian enemy to win her back. When the fleet is bound at Aulis by weather, the prophet Calchas informs Agamemnon that the goddess Artemis demands to be reconciled by the sacrifice of his daughter, Iphigeneia. The sacrifice is duly carried out (though, unbeknown to the mortal participants, Artemis saves Iphigeneia and installs her as her priestess at Tauris); the Greeks sail off to Troy; and Clytemnestra, unforgivingly embittered by the apparent slaughter of her eldest child, returns to Mycenae.

During Menelaus's absence, while Clytemnestra holds the stewardship of his kingdom, she is seduced by Aegisthus, who has his own reasons for hating the sons of his uncle Atreus and therefore fans the fires of her resentment. To remove any potential inconvenience or threat to her rule and her adultery, she sends her young son Orestes off to noble friends in Phocis, where he is raised in exile together with a friend, Pylades. Her other daughter, Electra (Aeschylus makes no mention of a third daughter, Chrysothemis, who has a significant role in Sophocles' *Electra*), is kept home at Mycenae in a state of virtual servitude and is not permitted to marry lest she bear a male child who might threaten the hegemony of Clytemnestra and Aegisthus.

The first play in the trilogy, *Agamemnon*, takes place on the day of

Agamemnon's return from ten years of war with the Trojans. Clytemnestra's brooding resolve to kill her husband for sacrificing
their daughter is strengthened by her jealous indignation at the fact
that he has brought back the prophetess Cassandra from Troy as his
courtesan. She lures him into the bath, where she stabs him as he
lies entangled in his robes, and then murders the captive Trojan
princess, as Aegisthus exults ecstatically over his vengeance. At this
point two of the three ordeals brought about by the curse of the
Atrides and cited by the chorus in the concluding summary of *The
Libation Bearers* (*Choêphori*) have taken place: the "child-eating dis-
tresses" ("paidoboroi mochthoi," 1068–69) of Thyestes; and the
"kingly sufferings" ("basileia pathê," 1070) of Agamemnon. The
third and final ordeal before the lifting of the curse provides the action of the second play.

ORESTES' HESITATION

The Libation Bearers takes place several years later. (The traditional
time for the joint rule of Clytemnestra and Aegisthus is seven years,
but Aeschylus leaves it unspecified.) Unlike the versions by Sophocles and Euripides, where Electra's manic fury provides the fiery focus and Orestes is reduced essentially to her agent, Aeschylus's
drama places Orestes squarely in the center of the action and of our
attention. Electra disappears entirely from the scene midway
through the play and long before the murders are carried out. (Her
last lines are spoken at 505–8, and Orestes addresses her directly
for the last time at 579–80.)[2] Orestes has reached an age on the
verge of manhood (he is presumably about eighteen years old) at
which he senses keenly that he has been not only deprived of the
right to mourn his father properly but also forced into exile and dispossessed of his rightful inheritance and kingdom. As the play
opens, Pylades has accompanied him back to Argos, where they approach Agamemnon's grave mound. We are made immediately
aware of Orestes' various motives for seeking vengeance on those
who have usurped his rights. (At this point the specific object of his
vengeance is still left undefined.) With his first words he appeals to

Hermes, as a god of the nether world (whose effigy presumably stands close to the grave site), to protect his forefathers' power and to aid him, the exile returned home. Praying then to his father, he offers a lock of his hair in tribute and utters words of mourning and salutation that he was not present to express when his father was murdered. As the chorus of black-robed women approaches, bearing libations for Agamemnon's grave, he catches sight of his grieving sister Electra and appeals to Zeus to stand by him in his effort to avenge his father's murder.

Within the first twenty lines, then, we know that Orestes has returned to Argos both to seek vengeance and to regain his rightful kingdom. (Since the opening lines are corrupt and incomplete, the initial monologue may originally have been somewhat longer.) Later these motives become pervasive. In the concluding dialogue with Clytemnestra, for instance, he berates her for sending him into exile so that she could enjoy her rule and her adultery with Aegisthus without interference (913ff.). In his joint prayer with Electra he appeals to his father to reinstate him in his rightful authority over their house (480). And he implores Zeus to raise his father's family once again to greatness from the insignificance to which it has sunk (262–63). In addition, he is hard-pressed by poverty because he has lost his inheritance (301).

While these various secular motives are clear from the outset, the most compelling incitement is revealed only after he has identified himself to Electra and the chorus (269ff.).[3] Orestes has been advised through an oracle by Apollo himself—he grew up in Phocis near the temple of Apollo at Delphi—to seek out and kill his father's murderers (who have still not been identified by name). We should note that Apollo does not himself call for blood vengeance: he simply points out to Orestes that avenging Erinyes have sprung from the spilled blood of his father—Furies who will not be satisfied until the murder is avenged and who will hound him, an exile, until he carries out his fated mission.[4] Accordingly, Apollo can tell him, on the one hand, that he must kill his father's murderers if he hopes to escape the Erinyes' pursuit and, on the other hand, promise him purification and liberation from the consequences of his deed. These, then, are the impulses that drive him on, Orestes summarizes: the god's behests, grief for his father, and sheer need (299ff.).

Orestes is no seasoned warrior like his father Agamemnon or the Trojan Aeneas. A member of a younger postwar generation, he is not motivated by the primitive lust for blood vengeance and, as far as we know, has never killed anyone. Moreover, as an exile educated in another country, he has a different perspective and a more detached view of the events in Argos.[5] Specifically, coming from the male-dominated realm of Phocis which pays homage to Apollo, he here encounters for the first time what is essentially a female-run society rendering tribute to the Erinyes and the gods of the underworld. Unlike Electra and the chorus, he has not been confronted every day since childhood with the consequences of his father's murder. Hence, even in the face of motives both secular and divine he is initially ambivalent.[6] Even though the oracles are persuasive, as he concedes to the chorus (297ff.), he is not fully persuaded. Nonetheless, the job still has to be done. In other words, he recognizes his responsibility intellectually but does not yet have a compelling moral commitment. He wants to regain his patrimony, but is not yet convinced that it is necessary to kill anyone to do so—certainly not his mother.

In his ambivalence, moreover, he is not fortified (as is Sophocles' Orestes) by the bacchantic fury of his sister Electra. Like Orestes, to be sure, she prays to Hermes and to her father to save their paternal house (123ff.) and to bring her brother home again. She must live like a slave, denied permission to marry, and Orestes must languish in exile while her mother with her paramour enjoys the usurped power and wealth of Agamemnon's kingdom. Yet she has no wish to descend to what she regards as her mother's moral squalor. When the chorus urges her to pray for a murdering avenger, she wonders how such a wish can be regarded as pious ("eusebê," 122) in the eyes of the immortals. A few lines later she expresses the hope that she may remain more chaste than her mother and that she may keep her hands pure (140–41)—that is, stay free of adultery and murder. And once her religious function at her father's tomb is completed, she vanishes into the women's quarters of the palace—the only suitable place for an unmarried daughter—when the process of revenge begins.[7]

It is left up to the chorus of enslaved freewomen, filled with hatred at their cruel and even godless ("dystheos," 525) mistress Clytemnestra, to whip up the children's fury; and in this capacity they amount to the spokeswomen of the Erinyes. Their opening parodos is governed by the general theme of revenge: the soil stained with blood breeds a lust for vengeance that can be satisfied only by the blood of the murderer. When Electra asks them to whom among her friends she can turn in her distress, they respond: to those who hate Aegisthus (110–11). Then they instruct her to call down some god or mortal avenger upon the murderers, who will punish them in kind (164). Persuaded by the chorus, Electra intersperses her prayers with curses. While the chorus is praying for a strong-speared liberator, Electra notices the lock of hair on the grave mound and footprints in the dust, both of which resemble hers. These clues, along with a patch of weaving, lead to her recognition of her brother, when he and Pylades step out from behind the tomb. (The criticism, and even ridicule, of this recognition scene by Euripides and later writers is irrelevant here.)

Orestes, who has overheard Electra's prayers and her conversation with the slave women, now recounts the Delphic oracle that has brought him home to Argos. In the remarkable and lengthy *kommos* that follows, which amounts to a collective conjuration of the dead Agamemnon,[8] the women of the chorus stir up the uncertain spirits of the two young siblings, reminding them that the goddess Dike is eager for vengeance and that three generations have already verified the saying that "the doer suffers" (310ff.).[9] Orestes and Electra, still hoping to find some other solution, appeal to their father in his grave and wish that he had been slain honorably at Troy. But the chorus, bringing them back to reality, insists on the need for earthly vengeance. The conflict between Apollo and the primitive deities of the underworld is most clearly manifest in the dialogue between Orestes and the chorus. It is an ancient law, they remind him, that blood spilled on the ground cries out for more blood (400–402). Only at this point, almost midway in the play, does it become clear to the children that their mother must die along with Aegisthus. While the chorus incites Orestes to ever greater rage by reminding him of the way his father's corpse was mutilated, Electra relates how she was shackled "like a dog" (446). Aware of his earlier ambivalence, the women urge Orestes to remain steadfast. Orestes and Electra, in turn, steel their resolve by appealing to their father's spirit and reminding him of the indignities he suffered in his murder. Indeed, through their incantations his spirit becomes virtually an invisible partner in the subsequent acts of revenge.

Yet Orestes still vacillates. Why, he wonders, did Clytemnestra suddenly, and for the first time since his murder, send the women out to the grave of her detested husband with libations? Had she experienced a change of heart? a sense of guilt perhaps? The chorus disillusions him. The queen had a nightmare in which she gave birth to a serpent that tore at her suckling breast, blending blood with her milk. She sent the women with libations in the hope of appeasing the dead. At this point Orestes finally accepts the inevitability that he has been cast in the role of the avenging serpent who must kill his mother. As the chorus chants its great ode on the passions that drive women to crime, Electra is sent back into the palace to prepare the way and distract attention while Orestes and Pylades plan their action.

Pretending to be merchants from Phocis, they announce themselves that evening at the palace gates and inform Clytemnestra of Orestes' alleged death: do his relatives wish his ashes brought back to Argos or buried abroad? Clytemnestra, who does not recognize her son after so many years, is shocked into grief by the unexpected news: she thought that she had sent Orestes far enough away to keep him free from the curse of the Atrides.[10] Welcoming the strangers into the palace, she sends a messenger, Orestes' former nurse, to summon Aegisthus. The nurse reports to the chorus women that Clytemnestra, despite her mournful mien, is secretly pleased by the news that another obstacle to her plans has been removed. Whether or not we credit the old woman's interpretation, Clytemnestra appears to be distrustful enough of the strangers to want Aegisthus to come with his armed bodyguard. But the chorus, persuading the nurse to omit that request from her message, chants its ode of justice and vengeance, ending with the exhortation to Orestes not to falter in his resolve, even when Clytemnestra appeals to him as her son, but to carry out his fated deed (829–31).

When Aegisthus arrives unaccompanied, the chorus women send him into the guest quarters of the palace, to hear for himself the news brought by the strangers from Phocia. Almost immediately they hear his cries from within, as Orestes—no hesitation here!— strikes him down. A servant rushes out, proclaiming Aegisthus's death and screaming for Clytemnestra. When Clytemnestra emerges and hears the news—that the dead are killing the living—, she immediately understands the riddle and the situation: she and Aegisthus are being undone by ruses similar to the ones they employed when they killed Agamemnon. We must admire Clytemnestra, a worthy opponent earlier of her husband and now of her son. She makes no attempt to deny her guilt. And although she knows from her recent dream that she is destined to die, she calls for her "man-slaying axe" (889), prepared to see who will win or lose this ultimate battle.

The doors to the guest quarters open to reveal Orestes standing over the body of Aegisthus. (With both Electra and Pylades out of the way for the moment, attention can be focused wholly on the climactic confrontation between mother and son.) "Now I'm looking for you," he tells her. "This one's done for" (892). When Clytemnestra expresses grief at Aegisthus's death, the indignant Orestes tells her that she can lie in the same grave. "You can't betray a dead man" (as she betrayed her husband Agamemnon). But when Orestes raises his sword, Clytemnestra—a woman whom we must imagine, like Dido, as radiant at the peak of womanly beauty and power—exposes her bosom, asking if he has no regard for the breast that nourished him. It is at this point that Orestes hesitates. Turning to his friend, he asks what he should do. "I'm ashamed to kill my mother" (899). This is Pylades' big moment, and he utters the only three lines allotted to him in the almost eleven hundred lines of the play. But they are enormously important lines because they remind Orestes of the divine oracle of Delphi. "What about Apollo's oracles, handed down to you by the Pythian priestess? What about your oaths? Make enemies of all mankind before antagonizing the gods!" (900–902).

Following this moment of hesitation, which has been called the "turning point"[11] and the moment of decision toward which the entire momentum of the work is directed,[12] the drama rushes toward its dénouement. Now that Orestes has been pressured into a decision, he is unmoved by Clytemnestra's further appeals and has a ready response for each of her skillful rhetorical thrusts. As the mother who nurtured him, she wants to spend her old age with her son; but he is appalled at the thought of living with the woman who killed his father. If it was Fate (*Moira,* 910) that caused Agamemnon's murder, then she should likewise hold Fate responsible for her imminent death. Has he no respect for a parent's curse? Not from a parent who cast him into misery. But she sent him to the house of friends! Yes, but he was sold as the son of a free man. For what price? He is ashamed to remind her that the price was the freedom to pursue her own adulterous affair with Aegisthus. But his father with his Trojan mistress wasn't all that innocent! Don't blame the man who was hard at work supporting her while she sat at home. Is Orestes determined to murder his own mother? She has brought about her own death. Does he not fear the wrath of a mother's curse? Less than that of his father, should he fail. Clytemnestra senses that her appeals are falling on ears as stony as Agamemnon's tomb. Indeed, he responds, because it was his father's fate that now determines hers. At this point she realizes that her own son is the serpent she foresaw in her fateful dream. Yes, he confirms as he drags her off to be slain beside the corpse of Aegisthus. "You killed one whom it was unrighteous to kill. Now you must yourself suffer a death that should not be" (930).

More than any other scene in the entire play, this episode with its rapid stichomythia exposes Clytemnestra's grim grandeur and Orestes' newly won manly decisiveness in their full force. There could be no true tragedy if Clytemnestra were presented simply as a murderous monster: she must engage our interest and respect, if not our sympathy. Without the maturity that transformed him from the youth of the prologue into the man of the final episodes, Ores-

tes would have been incapable of fulfilling his truly tragic destiny—
of avenging the murder of his father by killing his own mother. Here
for the first time on the stage of ancient Athens we encounter a con-
flicted, vacillating, hesitant hero.[13]

THE CONSEQUENCES

Orestes has carried out the murders expected of him by the code
of primitive blood vengeance and urgently advised by Apollo.[14]
What are the consequences? According to Homer's *Odyssey,* written
some four hundred years earlier at a time when blood vengeance
was still the prevailing customary law and moral code, Orestes'
killing of the adulterous usurper Aegisthus involves no blame or
pollution; rather, it brings great honor. (Homer does not make it
clear whether or not Orestes personally kills Clytemnestra.) Close
to the beginning of the epic, for instance, Athena encourages
Telemachus with the example of Orestes and the fame (*kleos*) he received for slaying his father's murderers (1.298–300). Sophocles'
Electra (composed between 418 and 410) is still virtually Homeric
in its archaic motivation. We have already noted that Sophocles' interest focuses on Electra and her furious lust for revenge—a focus
that predominates in European culture right down to Richard
Strauss's powerful operatic treatment. Sophocles' Orestes, who
apart from his brief initial appearance becomes a real participant
only two-thirds of the way into the play and acts out of purely personal motives (the need for blood vengeance), celebrates a political triumph and suffers no guilt or pursuit by the Erinyes.

Euripides wrote three plays dealing with Orestes. In his *Electra*
(roughly contemporaneous with Sophocles' version) it is again the
hate-filled sister who shares the center of action with her brother.
Yet both siblings emerge from the slaughter filled with remorse for
their deed. In an epilogue regarded by many scholars as a spurious
addition, she is married off to Pylades, and almost as an after-
thought we learn that Orestes is being pursued by the Erinyes.[15] But
the Dioscuri appear as *dei ex machina* and send Orestes to Athens,
with the promise that Athena will protect him from the onslaughts

of the Erinyes. His *Iphigeneia in Tauris* (ca. 412) is based on the legend according to which Iphigeneia was rescued from death at Aulis
by Artemis and taken to Tauris to serve as her priestess. Orestes goes
there with Pylades at the command of Apollo's ambiguously worded
oracle to rescue his sister (both Apollo's and Orestes') and to take
her back to Athens. In *Orestes* (ca. 408), finally, Euripides depicts
the events that take place a few days after the murder of Clytemnestra and Aegisthus. Orestes has gone mad and, together with Electra
and Pylades, has been sentenced to death by the citizens of Argos.
Eventually, however, Apollo appears to set matters straight: Electra
marries Pylades; Orestes must spend a year in exile but will then return to marry Helen's daughter Hermione. Apollo reconciles the
citizens of Argos with these resolutions.

The *Libation Bearers* ends with no such reassurances. When Orestes emerges from the palace, following the final ode in which the
chorus greets the breaking day, and displays the bodies of his victims along with the robes in which Clytemnestra once entangled
Agamemnon for the kill, he offers his deeds to be judged by Apollo,
god of the sun. He speaks almost dismissively of Aegisthus's death:
after all, the killing of an adulterer is traditionally justified by customary law (989–90). But he realizes that the murder of a mother,
whom once he loved but grew to hate, is a different matter altogether. In this issue he relies on the support of Apollo, who sent him
to Argos and whose command was reiterated by Pylades in his moment of hesitation. In an effort to convince himself of the right-
eousness of his deed—"Did she do it or did she not?" (1010)—he
contemplates the robe in which Agamemnon was slaughtered and
displays its bloody stains to the chorus. Now at last, with the robe as
witness, he can properly praise and mourn his avenged father.

At the same time, he has a moment of tragic awareness. For he
alone among the killers in his family has carried out his act of
vengeance with serious misgivings and without the impure motivation of his father's ambitious vanity (in sacrificing Iphigeneia) or
his mother's hatred and jealousy. He fulfills his fated and unavoid-
able duty but with regrets and remorse of conscience.[16] This is the
meaning of his concluding words: that he grieves for the deeds and
suffering of all involved since his very victory has brought him an

unenviable guilt (1016–17). Realizing that he is losing control of his mind, just as a charioteer loses control of his horses, he reiterates that he killed his mother "not without justice" (1027) and at the behest of Apollo, who had assured him that his act would be free of guilt. Contemplating the blood on his hands, he prepares to leave for Delphi, still an exile, half-dead and half-alive. The chorus seeks to reassure him, but suddenly Orestes cries out because he has just caught sight of the black-clad Erinyes, who—as exteriorizations of his own sense of guilt—remain invisible to all others: the "malignant hounds" of which his mother had spoken in the very same words (924 and 1054). It must be stressed that the Erinyes are not evil—neither those springing from Agamemnon's blood nor those now born of Clytemnestra's blood; they simply represent the old order of primitive morality which must be replaced by a new morality of justice.[17] As they converge on him, their eyes dripping with gore, he rushes out, leaving the chorus to wish him well. They also note that the third ordeal has now come to the House of Atreus and wonder where this hatred will end. (While the chorus is left unsure whether the family curse will ever cease, Aeschylus has hinted at a more optimistic future. His play, which begins in the fading day with appeals to Hermes, god of the underworld, closes in bright dawn with prayers to Apollo, god of light.)

THE DRAMATIC CONTEXT

The Libation Bearers, as we have seen, contains within itself adequate motives for the action and for Orestes' hesitation. Orestes has a justifiable claim to the patrimony that has been taken from him unrightfully; sent into exile and deprived of his heritage, he is in the embarrassing situation of dependence upon the generosity of others; he must witness the humiliation of his sister; his father has been dishonored by murder; his mother has taken an adulterous lover; under their tyrannical rule the kingdom of Argos has been ruthlessly oppressed. In addition to these wholly secular motives, he has been commanded by Apollo with the direst threats, but also with the promise of exculpation, to satisfy the customary expectation of blood vengeance for his father's murder. Finally, even his mother's fateful dream of the serpent birth has foretold his matricide. In all this he is aided and abetted by his sister and his best friend and incited by an often bacchantic chorus of slave women. Why should he not feel justified?

At the same time, after all Clytemnestra is his mother, whom he remembers fondly from his childhood.[18] His initial feelings of hatred and revenge are generalized ("the murderers") or displaced onto Aegisthus, the offending adulterer.[19] As an exile removed from the immediacy of the crime, he confesses his doubts to the chorus and seeks alternatives to the dread deed of matricide. When he first sees Clytemnestra after many years, she spontaneously utters words of grief over his alleged death. He kills Aegisthus first and without hesitation. But when he approaches his mother to carry out the final deed, he cannot fail to be impressed, if not persuaded, by her courage, her willpower, her intelligence—her beauty! So he experiences a moment of fateful hesitation, not unlike that of Aeneas weighing the pros and cons of slaying Turnus. But just as Pallas's sword-belt tips the balance for Aeneas, so too do Pylades' brief words remind Orestes of his obligation. So he turns to the work at hand—now matured by the intense experiences of the past hours, however, to a point at which he can match his mother's qualities of courage, will, and intelligence. In this sense he can indeed be said to contain in one character "the fullness of developing civilization."[20]

We can appreciate the full significance of Orestes' development only if we keep in mind that *The Libation Bearers* is the central play in a dramatic trilogy that begins with *Agamemnon* and goes on to *The Eumenides*. As *The Libation Bearers* ends, Orestes, crazed at the sight of the Erinyes who have been attracted by the blood on his hands, hurries off to seek purification through Apollo's healing touch. The action of *The Eumenides* begins at Delphi as the priestess of Apollo, having concluded her daily prayers, enters the temple and almost immediately rushes back out in horror to report that she has seen a suppliant sitting on the *omphalos*, his hands and his sword dripping with blood, and surrounded by a sleeping horde of hideous women. When the doors open to reveal the inner shrine, we recognize Orestes and the pursuing Erinyes, whom Apollo has charmed to sleep while he performs the ritual of purification. Although Orestes is purged of his pollution by the sacred rites and can once again come into contact with men and gods without contaminating them, Apollo warns that the Erinyes, goddesses of the underworld, will not be satisfied by this Olympian ritual, and advises him to travel to Athens to be judged and freed of their pursuit.

Following his departure the ghost of Clytemnestra appears and angrily rouses the Erinyes from their torpor. They quarrel furiously with Apollo, who promises to protect the matricide whom they swear to hound with their vengeance. Already at this early point we realize that the ancient blood feud of the Atrides, which hitherto has occurred as a purely human conflict, has erupted into a transcendental struggle between divine forces—the deities of the underworld and of the heavens, of matriarchy and patriarchy, of past and future.

The scene shifts to the temple of Athena on the Acropolis at Athens, where the Erinyes enter in hot pursuit of their victim. When Athena appears the Erinyes state their case and make what they regard as a legitimate and absolute claim on their victim as the murderer of his mother. (In Aeschylus, the Erinyes pursue only those who have killed blood relatives.) Orestes maintains that his deed was an act of justifiable homicide: a slaying, in short, which must be judged according to its motivation. (We now understand the importance of his purity of motive.) He asks Athena to decide whether or not he acted justly. The goddess, overwhelmed by the awesome responsibility of deciding between two equally persuasive arguments, decides to establish an altogether new institution to try the case: a jury of citizens.

Following a trial that closely adheres to the procedures of Athenian law and resorts to a Pythagorean genetic theory to prove that Orestes is not actually related by blood to Clytemnestra (because the male is the begetter and the female nothing but the vessel), Athena hands the case over to the jury. When it turns out that the votes are equally distributed, Athena rules (in accordance with Athenian law) in favor of the defendant, and Orestes is acquitted on the charge of homicide. Pledging an oath of peace with Athens,

Orestes returns to Argos to assume his rule. To Athena is left the task of assuaging the Erinyes, a task that she accomplishes with rhetorical sophistication, persuading the goddesses of the underworld to accept the new title of "Gracious Ones" (*eumenides*) and to take up their abode in Athens as its protective deities. Their new subterranean dwelling place beneath the Areopagus is a less-than-subtle reminder of their continued presence in Athenian culture—a repressed force that must be carefully controlled by governing reason and justice if it is not to burst forth again in its ancient fury.

The powerful courtroom dispute between the Erinyes and Apollo/Athena gives voice to a disagreement on two levels.[21] On the human level, it involves a conflict between the customary law of blood vengeance carried out by family or clan, which had prevailed unquestioned in the past, and the new institution of civil law enforced by society. (This transformation is reflected in Aeschylus's use of the much-cited Greek vocable *dikê*, which in the course of the trilogy shifts its meaning from "blood vengeance" to something closely approximating our modern sense of "justice.") On the divine level, it represents a contest between the ancient Mediterranean deities with their ties to the matriarchal underworld and a newer Hellenic hierarchy of Olympian deities and patriarchy.

In view of these shifts leading from the pure blood vengeance of *Agamemnon*—where Clytemnestra kills her husband (unrelated by blood) to avenge the murder of her daughter (related by blood as well as matriarchal ties)—to *The Eumenides*—where Orestes' killing of his mother (unrelated by blood, according to the Pythagorean theory) to avenge the death of his father (related by blood as well as patriarchal ties) is found justifiable by at least half the jury—we now understand Orestes' moment of hesitation in a new light, indeed, as momentous. Coming approximately at the midpoint of the trilogy, it exemplifies a point of equilibrium, of balance between two systems. The shift from the old gods to the new is hinted at by the appeals, in the opening passages, to Hermes, god of the underworld, and at the conclusion to Apollo, Olympian god of light. And the transition from blood vengeance to civil law is anticipated by Apollo's promise to Orestes that he will be redeemed for his deed.

Orestes, of course, is not clearly aware of the major social transformations that are taking place. But he plays a symbolic role in them, for they can take place only when individual men and women have come to question the iron law of blood vengeance and to shy away from its execution, turning instead to judgments based on justice. Orestes has no qualms about murdering Aegisthus, the adulterous schemer who has misappropriated his hereditary rights. But his hesitation before he slays Clytemnestra suggests, as does Aeneas's pause before he kills Turnus, that intuitively he questions the old ways, that a new sense of human love and compassion is struggling against the weight of the past and its traditions. The conflict between old and new gods, between ancient vengeance and new justice reflects, in turn, a shift in Greek history from tribal culture to civic society, from matriarchy to patriarchy, from private morality to social justice, from individual blood vengeance to the controlled legality of the city-state. For these reasons and others, Aeschylus's *Oresteia* has won a place not only as a literary masterpiece, but as a cornerstone of Western civilization for thinkers ranging from Nietzsche, Freud, and Jung to contemporary social anthropologists and legal historians, among others.[22] For reasons such as this William Arrowsmith remarked in a much cited essay that "the whole world and the fate of mankind hang in that moment of hesitation . . . for the play is about nothing less than the discovery of wisdom (*sophia*) under the yoke of awful necessity."[23] Yet any balanced reading of the trilogy and its reassuring conclusion must be constantly tempered by the thought of the Erinyes/Eumenides lurking, like a deeply repressed memory, in their cave beneath the Acropolis. Nietzsche had something similar in mind when he spoke, in *The Birth of Tragedy*, of the inevitable opposition of Dionysian and Apollonian elements in pre-Euripidean Greek tragedy.

THE HISTORICAL DIMENSION

Like Virgil, Aeschylus (ca. 525–456) also operates constantly with a "double perspective" focused on not only the mythic past but his own present as well.[24] He lived in a society in which the ancient mythic world-view was giving way to enlightened civilization.[25]

Though he wrote his trilogy (458 B.C.E.) some 450 years before Virgil composed the *Aeneid,* we can view the two works in Spengler's terminology as essentially simultaneous. Both poets were living historically in strikingly analogous periods of political turmoil as dictatorships yielded through the chaos of war to constitutional governments under ruthless demagogues and emperors.

Under the half-century rule of the tyrants Peisistratus and his son Hippias (561–510) Athens had developed from one among many minor Aegean city-states into a cultural center supported by prospering agriculture, manufacture, and commerce. Challenged in its political and economic might only by Sparta, it was becoming the focal point of archaic Greek culture. The art for which it has remained famous, however—the temple on the Acropolis, the gleaming statues, the red-figured vase painting, the poetry contests and dramatic performances—still stood principally in the service of religion.

During the first decades of the fifth century, following the ouster of the tyrants, striking changes took place. Athens emerged from the Persian Wars (490–479), in whose most famous battles Aeschylus fought, as the richest and most powerful empire of the Mediterranean world. The economic and political changes were accompanied by a constitutional process of democratization that had begun in 507 with the reforms of Cleisthenes. The postwar government under Pericles, Ephialtes, and their associates completed the process, dismantling the traditional hegemony of the Areopagus. (The violent conflict between old and new that these changes entailed is evident in both *The Eumenides* and Aeschylus's *Prometheus Bound.*)[26] As a member of the old aristocracy of Eleusis, Aeschylus was to a certain extent ambivalent about the reforms that, along with their improvements, also swept away many revered institutions.

The year 462 B.C.E. witnessed one of the most critical events in the history of Athenian democracy. Ephialtes, the leading spokesman of the people and a man with a reputation for incorruptibility and loyalty to the state, attacked the Council of the Areopagus, bringing suit against some of its members for alleged misconduct in office. He succeeded in stripping the Areopagus of most of its powers, which were transferred to more democratic entities. The

Areopagus retained little more than its ancient charge of trying cases of homicide and the supervision of various cultic affairs. Ephialtes himself was assassinated within a year by his aristocratic opponents. We can hardly appreciate today the civic trauma that these events produced: the social and political balance between classes achieved by the previous isonomy was upset as the nobility lost power in the new democracy. For the first time in history, the polis was ruled by the people, and not by tyrants or the nobility.

It was under the immediate impression of such events that Aeschylus composed, in the next few years, his *Oresteia* trilogy.[27] Today it is not difficult to see that Orestes' hesitation reflects not only the archaic transition in the years following the Trojan War from the law of blood vengeance to the new justice of civil society and not only the human impulse toward love and mercy, but also the uncertainties of mid-fifth-century Athenians confronted with a seismic shift in their own society in the struggle between the aristocracy and the polis, between traditional and modern systems of law and government, between old values and a new morality.

THE TROJAN DILEMMA

Despite the 450 years that separate them, we can therefore regard Aeneas and Orestes as contemporaries. Indeed, since both their actions take place in the eighth year after the fall of Troy, we can almost imagine the raised swords, the moment of hesitation, and the fatal blow occurring simultaneously in Argos and on the Hesperian coast. Although they belong to different generations—Aeneas must be approximately the same age as Orestes' murdered father—both heroes face essentially the same dilemma: they are trying to escape the burden of a past represented by the claims of blood vengeance into a new world governed by law and justice. In each case, that future has been prophesied to them by voices from the beyond—by Anchises from the "blissful groves" of the blessed dead, and by Apollo through his Delphic oracle. Given the difference in their age and experience, of course, each confronts the dilemma in a different way: one by reverting and the other by succumbing.

Aeneas, belonging to the war generation, reverts momentarily to the traditional moral code, unable in his fury to sustain the vision of the future Roman *imperium* adumbrated by his father in the underworld. Orestes is a member of the postwar cohort, for whom blood vengeance is history, not personal experience; yet he succumbs to it momentarily even as he unconsciously longs for the future society of justice foretold by Apollo. So they hesitate, torn between past and future, until they are reminded of duty and necessity by friends in the form of Pallas's belt and Pylades' brief words. Their hesitation reflects, as well, the conflict between old gods and new. Just as Aeneas is caught in the conflict between Juno and Athena until Jupiter banishes the dark powers of the underworld and opens the way to the Roman future, so too Orestes is torn between the Erinyes' cry for blood vengeance and Apollo's protective aegis until Athena tames the dark powers of primitive morality into Eumenides and makes possible the new legal society of Athens.

Hitherto we have spoken only of the two hesitant heroes. But their victims also display certain common traits. First, both Clytemnestra and Turnus adhere to the older "pre-Trojan" way of thinking that Orestes and Aeneas are trying to escape. In their ruthlessness (Clytemnestra's murder of Agamemnon and Cassandra and Turnus's bloody rampages on the battlefield) they could almost be mother and son—certainly more so than Clytemnestra and Orestes. Beyond that, they are linked by their superstitious belief in fate and omens. Clytemnestra wakes up, screaming in horror, from her nightmare of the serpent to which she has given birth—a dream so frightening that it causes her, for the first time since the murder of Agamemnon eight years earlier, to send libations to his grave in the hope of appeasing the spirits of the dead. When she recognizes in Orestes the fulfillment of that ominous vision—those are her very last words in the play—, she lets herself fatalistically be drawn inside to her death. Similarly Turnus does not lose his spirits and courage until Jupiter sends down one of the Dirae who, transformed into an owl, flies at Turnus and, shrieking, beats its wings on his shield. "At this, a numbness dissolved his limbs in fear, his hair bristled in terror, and his voice stuck in his throat" ("illi membra novus solvit formidine torpor, / arrectaeque horrore comae et vox faucibus haesit," 12.867–68). Their susceptibility to ancient superstitious fears ultimately makes Clytemnestra and Turnus vulnerable to the death blows of their killers.

Aeschylus and Virgil, as we have noted, were writing at analogous times in the history of their own civilizations—during transitional periods, namely, when myth was giving way to history, religion to justice, and violence to law. The two poets share another characteristic: both cultivated a literary style of enormous compression, in which often the most complex thoughts and emotions are conveyed in a few tightly packed words. (Virgil's "sunt lacrimae rerum" [*Aen.* 1.462] is one of the best-known examples.) Accordingly, as in the case of the two crucial moments of hesitation, a great deal is left unsaid and must be filled in from context and by interpretation. Yet, as we have seen, both poets used the mythic past of the transitional years immediately following the Trojan War as a mirror of their own societies. The moments of hesitation summon our attention at crucial points of two great world masterpieces—in the last lines of the *Aeneid* and in the middle of the *Oresteia*—to the eternal tension between myth and history, between religion and law, between violence and justice, whether at the time of the Trojan War, in fifth-century Athens, in first-century Rome, or in the global world in the first decade of the twenty-first century.

3

Parzival, or Silence at Munsalvaesche

Readers approaching the medieval romances of the quest for the Holy Grail would do well first of all to put out of mind the jumble of motifs familiar to many from Wagner's *Parsifal*. Opera fans will recall the second scene of act one, which is set in a mythic realm where time has become space ("zum Raum wird hier die Zeit"). During the entire scene, while the grievously wounded Amfortas sings interminably about his suffering, both physical and spiritual, to the counterpoint of his anguished father Titurel, and while the Grail magically produces wine and bread for the entire company, Parsifal loiters for half an hour in a spellbound trance on the periphery, uttering not a sound. When Amfortas has been carried back out and the knights have departed in solemn procession, Gurnemanz shoves him out the door in disgust, muttering "You're nothing but a fool!"

Wagner offers no explanation for Parsifal's behavior or for Gurnemanz's frustration. We know from the opening scene that the inhabitants of Wagner's exclusively male (as well as vegetarian and racist) Kingdom of the Grail are awaiting the arrival of "a pure fool, enlighted by compassion" ("durch Mitleid wissend / der reine Thor"), but he has given us no hint what the savior is supposed to do.[1] Not until the conclusion of the almost five-hour opera are we

54

acquainted with his mission. In the second act Parsifal recovers
from Klingsor the holy spear that the magician had long ago stolen
from Amfortas, wounding him in the process, and that alone can
heal the wound. At the end of act three Parsifal finally accomplishes
the deed by touching Amfortas's wound with the tip of the spear—
a deed so astonishing that it causes the deceased Titurel to sit up
momentarily in his coffin while the enchantress Kundry sinks dead
to the ground. As a white dove descends from above in benediction
of the new King of the Grail, all join in a hymn of praise for the miracle of healing and salvation.

We never learn why, if the recovery of the holy spear is necessary
for the general redemption, Parsifal is blamed in the first act, long
before he has heard the legend of the spear and won it back from
Klingsor. Enthralled by the incantatory power of the music, we readily overlook this and other inconsistencies of Wagner's libretto.
(Even Wagner's spelling of the hero's name, Parsifal, is a corruption based on his spurious belief in the Persian origins of the legend.) But a quick glance at either of the principal medieval
sources—Chrétien de Troyes' *Conte du Graal* or Wolfram von Eschenbach's *Parzival*—quickly clarifies the mystery. For there it is
not the touch of the lance that heals the wound; the lance is present in the Grail Castle the entire time. It is the question of simple
human compassion which the hero in his ignorance fails to ask the
king of the Grail at their first encounter: "What's wrong with you?"

PARZIVAL'S HESITATION

We shall take as our text Wolfram's *Parzival* (completed ca. 1210),
which is both complete and psychologically more fully developed
than his source, Chrétien's fragmentary *Conte du Graal*. Our analysis will have no need to deal with many issues that have concerned
the specialists for more than a century: Wolfram's sources (Chrétien? an otherwise unknown Provençal writer named Kyot?);[2] the
meaning of the grail (Old French *graal*; Middle High German
grâl)—chalice of the Last Supper or, as Wolfram has it, simply a
magical stone? or its origins (Celtic? Arabic?);[3] the complicated

time relationships of the plot and their connections to liturgical and astrological calendars;[4] the theology of the work, including the mystery of the Neutral Angels;[5] or such biographical matters as Wolfram's education (literate or unlettered?) and his relationship to his contemporary literary competitors.[6] It has been estimated that in the past century Wolfram has elicited more scholarly commentary than any other German poet apart from Goethe.

When Parzival arrives in Terre de Salvaesche and meets the gentleman fishing at the beginning of book 5 (224.1 ff.), we already know a great deal about him, but nothing whatsoever about the grail.[7] (This is in contrast to Wagner's opera, where we learn about Amfortas's wound, the theft of the lance by Klingsor, and the sorry situation at the Grail Castle long before Parsifal enters the scene.) Parzival is the son of King Gahmuret and Queen Herzeloyde, rulers of the kingdoms of Anschouwe, Waleis, and Norgals. Gahmuret— who (in bks. 1 and 2) has already sired an older son, the speckled Feirefiz, from the black queen Belacane of Zazamanc—is killed before the walls of Baghdad, fighting for his friend and former liegelord Baruc. Receiving the news, Herzeloyde disposes of her wealth and kingdoms and retreats with a few trusted servants into the forests of Soltane, forbidding her men and women ever to speak of "knighthood" in the presence of her child, lest he follow in the path of his father and suffer a similar early death. So Parzival is raised as a true simpleton (*tor*) in the tradition of *Dümmling* folktales—in ignorance of his father, his family, his heritage, even his own name—but skilled as a huntsman and aesthetically sensitive to the sweet sounds of the birds.[8] (Already here he displays a susceptibility to trancelike states induced by natural phenomena, which we witness years later when he falls into a trance at the sight of three drops of blood in the snow.) His formal instruction in religion is equally neglected although his mother leads an exemplary Christian life: she tells him only that God is brighter than the day (119.19) while the lord of Hell is black and treacherous, lacking the primary knightly quality *triuwe* ("loyalty," or "trustworthiness"). Accordingly, when in his teens he encounters four knights in resplendent armor, he thinks in his simple-minded literalness that they are gods. When they inform him laughingly that they are only knights, he urgently inquires how one becomes a knight. From King Arthur, they tell him, surmising from his radiant if ragged beauty his noble heritage.

When Parzival reports to his chagrined mother that he has seen four knights clad more brilliantly even than God, he pleads with her to permit him to seek out King Arthur and to obtain knightly honors for himself. With a heavy heart she gives her consent, but not without sharing with him four random bits of advice, which the simple youth takes literally to heart: cross streams only where the water is clear; greet everyone courteously; accept gratefully the advice of any experienced gray-haired man willing to give it; and seize every opportunity to take a lady's kiss and her ring. On the following morning, clad in the fool's garb in which his mother—consistent with the *Dümmling* theme—has dressed him, he sets off in such high excitement that he fails to notice that Herzeloyde falls dead of sorrow behind him.

The next day, having followed a stream to a clear and shallow ford, he sees a beautiful noblewomen asleep beneath a tent. Heeding his mother's words in the most literal sense, he leaps upon the lady, stealing both her kisses and her ring—an act that subsequently provokes dire consequences for the lady Jeschute with her husband. Later he comes upon another woman, grieving over her dead lover, who turns out to be his cousin Sigune. Recognizing him from his words, she reveals to him his name and his heritage. The next day, passing on the way a knight whose splendid red armor arouses his desire, he finally arrives at King Arthur's court. Impressed with the youth's appearance, despite the fool's garments with which his mother has outfitted him, Arthur promises to equip him as a knight. But Parzival, impatient, demands the armor of the Red Knight he has seen outside. Putting aside any fears for the lad's safety, Arthur tells him that he may have it if he can win it. Despite his inexperience and to everyone's astonishment, Parzival succeeds in killing the knight with his javelin—the first and only killing that he will commit—and strips the knight of his armor.

Accoutered in his new finery, Parzival arrives that evening at the castle of Prince Gurnemanz, described as a "captain of courtesy" ("houbetman der wâren zuht," 162.23). Recognizing the youth's quality despite his rough ways, the elderly Gurnemanz takes him under his tutelage for two weeks and teaches him the rules of knightly and courtly culture, which Parzival takes as literally to heart as earlier his mother's precepts: to practice compassion, humility, and moderation; to be manly and brave; to spare those he has defeated in battle (like Aeneas); to cleanse himself from the rust and grease of weapons after battle so that he may be attractive to women; and, fatefully, not to ask many questions ("ir ensult niht vil gevrâgen," 171.17). With these lessons in mind, Parzival rides off to the kingdom of Brobarz, where he liberates the beleaguered city of Belrepeire from its besiegers and wins the hand of its queen, the beautiful Condwiramurs (bk. 4). After a time, however, he takes leave of his beloved wife in order to visit his mother and go in search of further knightly adventure.

Arriving at a lake, Parzival asks directions from a handsomely clad gentleman who appears to be fishing (bk. 5). The fisherman sends him to his nearby castle, promising to receive him later that evening. Parzival is welcomed by a crowd of knights young and old, who relieve him of his arms, provide him with water for washing, and bring him fresh garments. Even though both the kingly fisherman and his knights are "sorrowful" ("trûreg," 225.18 and 228.26), Parzival is well treated and invited to the evening meal. (We may leave aside as irrelevant here the brief and controversial episode of the "speech-ready" man, who has been regarded as a jester or as a knight overcome with emotion.)[9] And now we reach Parzival's moment of hesitation (229.23ff.).

The dinner is anything but a festive occasion. His host, seated despite the warm season before a roaring fire and clad in heavy garments, invites Parzival to sit beside him. Immediately a page rushes in bearing a lance bloody at its tip, whereupon everyone in the vast hall weeps and wails in lamentation. Carrying the lance around the perimeter of the walls, the page rushes back out again. Then a great door is thrown open, and a procession of twenty-four handsomely clad ladies and maidens enters, bearing ivory table legs, a table top of precious stone, candles, and a pair of silver knives. Finally the queen, Repanse de Schoie, enters bearing "the wish of paradise"— "a thing called the grail" ("daz was ein dinc, daz hiez der grâl,"

235.23)—and places it before the king. The four hundred knights, seated at a hundred tables and served by almost twice that number of pages, receive from the wondrous *grâl*, each according to his desire, food both hot and cold and refreshments of every kind.

Parzival sits quietly and curiously observes these wonders, yet—in keeping with the courtly precepts learned from Gurnemanz—doesn't say a word ("durch zuht in vrâgens doch verdrôz," 239.10). If he remains here as long as he stayed with Gurnemanz, he reflects, then surely his questions will eventually be answered. At this point a page brings in a handsome sword. Telling Parzival that he had often borne the sword into battle before God devastated his body, the king presents it to him. But again Parzival restrains his questions out of courtesy. Following these incidents the tables are cleared away again, the gathering disperses, and Parzival is led to his bedchamber.

The next morning, awaking from sorrowful dreams, Parzival is astonished to discover that the castle is deserted. He dresses himself, finds his horse and weapons, and rides out of the castle. Suddenly a page, raising the drawbridge behind him, curses Parzival for neglecting to ask his host the question that would have brought him a great reward. A short time later he again encounters his cousin Sigune, who informs him that he has been at Munsalvaesche, the castle of the Grail, and that its lord is Amfortas, who, so grievously wounded that he can neither ride nor walk nor lie nor stand, must spend his time in a leaning position. She takes it for granted that Parzival asked the question that would have brought him all he could desire here on earth. Dismayed to learn of his omission, she too curses him and spells out the terms of his mission: You should have taken pity on your host, on whom God has displayed his wondrous power, by asking about his suffering!" ("iuch solde iuwer wirt erbarmet hân, / an dem got wunder hât getân, / und hetet gevrâget sîner nôt," 255.17–19). Though Parzival is still alive, he has lost all hope of heavenly bliss (*saelde*) and knightly honor (*êre*).

Departing in sadness from Sigune, Parzival makes his way via various encounters and adventures back to King Arthur's court, where he is now formally invited to become a knight of the Round Table. But as he enjoys the felicities of the knights and ladies, the hideously ugly sorceress Cundrie appears and warns King Arthur that the fame of the Round Table has been blemished by the presence of Parzival, who brought sorrow on the fisherman by his lack of compassion and, by his silence, great sin upon himself ("dâ erwarp iu swîgen sünden zil," 316.23). With all the rhetorical power at her command—she is gifted enough to speak all languages, including Latin, Arabic, and French—she curses Parzival (for the third time, after the page at the castle gate and Sigune) elaborately and inventively and condemns him to Hell ("gein der helle ir sît benant," 316.7) before riding off as abruptly as she had appeared.

Parzival tries to explain to the knights and ladies his behavior at Munsalvaesche, recalling that Gurnemanz had advised him to avoid bold questions ("vrêvellîche vrâge," 330.5). Saying that nothing is more important to him than to win back his honor and their esteem, he takes his leave. His new friend Gawan, Arthur's nephew, wishes that God may help him in his quest, but Parzival asks the same question he had put years earlier to his mother: What is God? Were he almighty, he would not have brought Parzival such shame. Although up to this point he has sought to serve God, he now abjures that service. With these bitter and despondent words Parzival rides away from the King Arthur's court and, for the time being, out of the narrative, which for the next two books turns to the adventures of Gawan.

Here we should pause to recapitulate. Parzival's omission—his failure to ask the question—differs from the earlier cases of hesitation that we have considered. To be sure, it involves a word rather than a deed—and a word of salvation at that, rather than an act of killing. Yet it is no less a moment of hesitation with consequences that last far longer than the few moments or minutes required by Aeneas and Orestes to consider their respective dilemmas. For on this occasion Parzival is not given the opportunity to complete his act. Following his hesitation the entire entourage of the Grail Castle disappears, and only after four and a half years of deliberation has Parzival matured sufficiently to be admitted again into the presence of Anfortas, where he can finally und unhesitatingly complete the initially inhibited act. Again the moment of hesitation amounts to an inhibition whose causes have been made amply clear by the preceding episodes. Up to the moment of his encounter with

Gurnemanz, Parzival had never hesitated to ask questions. What is God? What is a knight? Who can grant me knighthood? It is only Gurnemanz's precept, which in his naiveté Parzival takes as literally as he had earlier taken his mother's teachings, that prevents him from giving expression to the natural curiosity and sympathy he feels at the sight of the bloody lance, the wonders of the grail, and Anfortas's obvious agony. "Parzival noted well the splendor and the great wonder: but his good breeding prevented him from asking" (239.8–10). Parzival's behavior thus constitutes a textbook case of inhibition through the imposition of civilized order at the social level. Here, however, in contrast to the hesitations of Aeneas and Orestes, the civilizing influence is not rejected in a reversion to basic instincts; instead, it maintains its authority, causing Parzival to behave in a manner contrary to his natural impulses.

Why should such an innocent omission be regarded as a failure of *triuwe* (Sigune at 255.15) or even as sin (Cundrie at 316.23)? Various reasons have been suggested.[10] Some scholars have spoken of Parzival's fall from innocence through the killing of the Red Knight. Some have cited the self-centeredness, the lack of ethical maturity, which let him desert his mother, pounce on the lady Jeschute, and ignore the grief of his cousin Sigune. Others have pointed to his superficial understanding of knighthood, which at this point is still focused on such externalities as rules of behavior and glittering armor (of the four knights at the beginning, of the Red Knight). Still others blame the emotional immaturity that prevents him from making autonomous decisions. And we must keep in mind the folktale element underlying the plot, which often involves magical questions and requires such a failure if the story is not to end at this point.

Unlike Wagner's opera, then, Wolfram's *Parzival* offers an abundance of reasons for the hero's behavior, whether we call it sin, *untriuwe,* or naive adherence to social rules. Unlike Wagner, moreover, Wolfram has as yet provided no explanation for the situation at Munsalvaesche, the meaning of the bloody spear and the grail itself, or the reactions of the other participants. We have been given one side of the social equation: the courtly/knightly life represented by the adventures of Parzival's father Gahmuret in books 1 and 2, from which Herzeloyde flees in vain, but which is discovered and pursued by Parzival in books 3 and 4 until finally, in book 6, he is accepted at the Round Table as a fully qualified knight. For a full explanation of the grail cult, the other side of the epic world of *Parzival,* however, we must wait until book nine.

THE MYSTERIES OF MUNSALVAESCHE

The tale now turns to the adventures of Gawan, in which the Red Knight is sighted only now and then on the periphery. Not until book 9 does Wolfram—presumably in response to the queries and demands of his listeners—return to Parzival, reminding us that he was chased away from the Round Table and in search of the grail by Cundrie and her "unsweet words." In the meantime, Parzival has roamed widely on land and sea in the attempt to regain his honor and win fame. Finally, after yet another encounter with his cousin Sigune, who tells him that the Castle of the Grail is not far away, he meets an elderly knight, who informs him that the day is Good Friday. Parzival rides on, thinking that God, if he truly rewards those who have striven with knightly merit, will perhaps come to his aid today. He arrives at Fontane la Salvaesche, the abode of the hermit Trevrizent, from whom Parzival now finally learns the mysteries of Munsalvaesche.

Trevrizent, it emerges, is the brother not only of Anfortas and Repanse de Schoye, but also of Herzeloyde—and therefore the uncle of Parzival, who is thus related to the family in charge of the grail. The grail, he recounts, was left on earth by the Neutral Angels—it is a matter of considerable scholarly dispute as to whether the grail was brought to earth or simply found there by them—, who turned it over for safekeeping to Titurel, who bequeathed it by way of his son Frimutel to his grandson Anfortas. When Trevrizent tells his nephew that it has been four and a half years since he passed that way following his first visit to Munsalvaesche, Parzival confesses that he has since that time entered no church, blaming God for all his troubles. Trevrizent, by far the most encyclopedically learned figure in the epic romance, gives him a quick lesson in Christian theology and on the nature of God, whereupon Parzival expresses a desire to regain his faith, claiming that he longs for the grail even more than for his wife. Trevrizent tells him how the company of the grail live from the stone, which restores health and vitality and provides the Templars with all their dietary needs. It acquires its power by means of a white dove, which annually on Good Friday delivers a wafer from heaven and leaves it on the stone. The names of those who are summoned to serve the grail are announced by an inscription that appears on the edge of the stone and then immediately disappears again. Only one man, he continues, ever found his way there unbidden: "an ignorant man, who went away in sin because he didn't speak to his host about the grief in which he saw him" (473.13–16).

Parzival is not yet prepared to confess his guilt. Instead, he tells the story of his own life, whereby further family connections emerge—Parzival is related through his father to King Arthur and through his mother to Anfortas—along with the facts that the Red Knight whom Parzival killed at the beginning of his adventures was his cousin and that his mother Herzeloyde died of grief at Parzival's departure. Parzival's uncle, Anfortas, Trevrizent continues, is king of the Grail and, as such, is forbidden to seek any love other than that specified by the writing on the stone. In his youth, however, he went against the rules of the order and, while jousting in honor of his lady, was wounded in the testicles by a poisoned lance. Although a physician removed the lance head, the wound festered so severely that it could be cured by none of the remedies known to the medieval world. The pain can be temporarily relieved by inserting the tip of the lance into the wound, whereby the heat of the poison draws the frost from his body. But this matter hardens on the lance tip so solidly that it can be removed only by the two silver knives. Because the wound's stench is so terrible that Anfortas must cleanse himself daily in the lake, he has come to be known as "the fisherman." Hence Anfortas's suffering, and hence Trevrizent's own decision to give up knighthood and become a hermit, living for his brother's salvation.

At this point, finally, his narrative comes to the moment of Parzival's first arrival at Munsalvaesche. A message had appeared on the grail that a knight would come and, if he asked a specific question— "My lord, what causes your distress?" ("herre, wie stêt iuwer nôt?"

484.27)—the king would be healed. Should anyone forewarn the visitor, the results would fail. But should he be successful, he would inherit the kingdom and become the new king of the Grail. The visitor failed—out of *tumpheit* (youthful naiveté or simpleminded ignorance). Parzival still cannot bring himself to confess his sin. They forage for their food, wash before their meal, and feed Parzival's horse. Finally Parzival admits to his uncle that the visitor to Munsalvaesche was none other than he.

Trevrizent is dismayed. Parzival was betrayed by his five God-given senses, he says, which should have alerted him to the significance of the sights, sounds, smells, tastes, and feelings offered to him at the Castle of the Grail. On that night, because of the peculiar conjunction of the planets, Anfortas's pain was greater than usual and had to be relieved by the lance; it was his blood that Parzival had seen on the bloody lance; the lamentation that went up around the vast hall was a general response to the agony suffered by their king. Parzival must now add that sin of omission to his two other involuntary sins—responsibility for the death of his mother and the killing of his cousin Ither.

Parzival remains for two weeks with his uncle, who finally absolves him from the sins of which—albeit unwittingly—he is guilty. The absolution is possible because, at this point, Parzival through his own spiritual suffering has reached the emotional maturity and moral integrity to accept his responsibility and to express remorse for his sins. In other words, he has begun the process of internalizing the religious and knightly values that hitherto he had respected in a superficial and purely mechanical manner. Like Orestes at Delphi, he has undergone the religious ritual of purification and must now submit to the civic judgment. But redemption does not come so quickly. Again his story is interrupted at a crucial point by the narrative of Gawan's adventures.

THE SEQUEL

Gawan's adventures in books 10–14 revolve around the Castle Marvelous (*Schastel Marveile*), which amounts to a secularized and inverted parallel to Munsalvaesche.[11] Cast under a spell by the magician Clinschor, it too is a place of sadness, where the knights and ladies live in a state of human isolation and deprivation of love. Like Anfortas, Clinschor suffers from a wound in the groin, having been castrated by an infuriated husband whose wife he seduced. And like the Castle of the Grail it also features a wonder: a magic pillar that works like a telescope, enabling the viewer to see what is happening at great distances. As a result of Clinschor's spell, the inhabitants of Schastel Marveile can be liberated only by the knight who succeeds in surviving the ordeal of the magic bed, which is protected by five hundred slings and stones, five hundred crossbows and bolts, and a huge guardian lion. Gawan masters the various trials and, in the process, succeeds in winning the love and the hand of the haughty Orgeluse, whose beauty originally brought about Anfortas's downfall. At this point Gawan encounters an unknown knight, who almost slays him in battle before their identities are revealed—and Parzival is spared the sin of killing yet another kinsman. Their reunion is celebrated at a great festivity with King Arthur's followers.

Soon after his departure from Gawan, Parzival encounters an infidel knight in the fields below, with whom he wages the fiercest battle he has ever fought and by whose might he is almost overcome. When Parzival's sword breaks, however, the noble stranger refuses to take advantage of him. In their ensuing conversation it emerges that he is none other than Parzival's older brother Feirefiz, who has come with twenty-five armies and fantastic riches from his oriental kingdom of Zazamanc to the western lands in search of his father Gahmuret. They ride back to Arthur's encampment, where their reunion, already witnessed through the magical telescopic pillar at Schastel Marveile, and Feirefiz's introduction to the Round Table are grandly celebrated. Suddenly the sorceress Cundrie rides up bearing the grail insignia of turtledoves. Welcoming Feirefiz, she announces to Parzival that his name has again appeared in an epigraph on the grail: he is to be king of Munsalvaesche, where his wife Condwiramurs is to join him. (This is important: because her name appears on the stone as his destined wife, Parzival is able to avoid a fate similar to that of poor Anfortas, who sought an impermissible love.) Having expiated his earlier sins, he is now given a second opportunity to put the healing question to Anfortas. Following three days of celebrations and the exchange of costly gifts, Parzival and Feirefiz ride off with Cundrie.

The sixteenth and final book is almost anticlimactic since we have already learned the foregone conclusion. (Wolfram leaves it unexplained why the question still retains its magical force since, originally, it was supposed to be asked only at first encounter and would be rendered impotent if anyone betrayed its meaning.) Escorted by the sorceress, the two brothers arrive at Munsalvaesche, where the ailing Anfortas, against his wishes, has been kept alive by his weekly exposure to the grail and where the air must be sweetened with fragrant herbs to allay the stench of his wound. After the mournful king has greeted the two brothers, Parzival kneels three times in the direction of the sacred stone and then, turning to Anfortas, poses the at-this-point purely ceremonial question: "oeheim, waz wirret dir?" ("Uncle, what ails you?" 795.29). From this moment on, things move very quickly. Instantly Anfortas is restored to his full health and radiant beauty, and Parzival is recognized by the knights of Munsalvaesche as their king and lord.

Parzival rides out to convey the joyous news to his uncle Trevrizent in the nearby hermitage. Then he gallops on to meet the entourage escorting Condwiramurs and their two sons, whom he has never seen, from distant Brobarz. Making over all his lands to his infant son Kardeiz and entrusting him to guardian knights, Parzival and Condwiramurs take the other son, Loherangrin, with them as their successor at Munsalvaesche. At a great celebration the grail is again brought in by Repanse de Schoye and set before the new king and queen.

Feirefiz is mystified at the proceedings because, as an infidel, he is unable to perceive such a sacred Christian miracle as the Holy Grail; but he is smitten with love for Repanse de Schoye. Following his baptism the next day, however, he wins both her hand in marriage and the ability to see the wondrous stone. After twelve days of festivities, they return to his lands in the East, where Repanse de Schoye bears a son named John, later to be known as Prester John.[12] Following a succinct recapitulation of the later life of Parzival's son Loherangrin, Wolfram concludes the 24,810 verses of his epic romance with the observation:

swes leben sich sô verendet,
daz got niht wirt gephendet
der sêle durch slîbes schuld,
und der doch der werlde hulde
behalden kan mit werdekeit,
daz ist ein nütziu arbeit.

(827.19–24)

(If a man ends his life in such a way that God is not cheated of his soul
by fault of his body, and still can retain the world's respect with dig-
nity, that is a useful life goal.)

THE HESITATION RE-VIEWED

If the concluding aphorism, suggesting an ideal synthesis of the religious with the knightly life, summarizes the meaning of the work,
we can now look back and see Parzival's hesitation during his first
visit to Munsalvaesche in a new light. We have already explored the
reasons in his life up to that point which inhibited him initially: his
inexperience, his still-childish egocentricity, and above all his literal
adherence to the precepts handed down by his mother and Gurnemanz.[13] But now we see that his hesitation is not merely a psychological phenomenon. Larger issues are also at play, both personal
and social.

In a very central sense, the meaning of Wolfram's epic romance
can be viewed as a development from the opening aphorism to the
concluding one.

Ist zwîvel herzen nâchgebûr,
daz muoz der sêle werden sûr.

(1.1–2)

(If doubt or uncertainty resides within one's heart, it will be bitter for
the soul.)

Already in these opening lines the theme of doubt and uncertainty—that is to say, the clash of different viewpoints or feelings—
is anticipated.[14] Parzival's process of *Bildung*, we understand, will
lead him from doubt to certainty, from conflict to the resolution of

opposing viewpoints. This development embraces of course the emotional tension between instinct and courtesy that inhibits Parzival's question on his first visit to Munsalvaesche. But it also anticipates the contest between the two great ways of life that are reconciled at the end of the narrative. These oppositions are symbolized by the Round Table and the Grail; and they are embodied, for all their human flaws, in Arthur and Anfortas; they are also exemplified ideally in the persons of Gawan, the paragon of knighthood, and Trevrizent, the profound spokesman of Christian faith and understanding. The possibility of their reconciliation begins to emerge, at least in the reader's mind, from the moment in his conversations with Trevrizent when Parzival learns that, unlike any other figure in the enormous work, he is related by blood to all these men and hence to both institutions. Parzival, in short, emerges as the living synthesis of the two ways of life, of knighthood and religion.[15] Wolfram's meaning, however, is continually shaded by a complexity and denseness of language of a quality that matches what we have already noted in Aeschylus and Virgil.

If we look back at the story from the concluding aphorism, we may now see Parzival's mission in its largest sense as the ultimate reconciliation of these ideals as he moves from *tumpheit,* from his childish ignorance and naiveté, to combine the roles known to the medieval world as *caput mundi* and *caput ecclesiae.* Both knighthood and religion enter his life at an early point. But the religion that he learns from his mother—simply that God is brighter than the day and loves everyone—is no less shallow than his initial conception of knighthood, which amounts to little more than the desire for shining armor and the most superficial application of Gurnemanz' precepts. His lack of true understanding—compassion for others and restraint vis-à-vis one's enemies—leads him into his first impulsive sins: the violation of Jeschute, the unfeeling dismissal of the mourning Sigune, and the killing of the Red Knight. As he matures and internalizes the ideals of knighthood and religion, he moves from his initial role as pure outsider—symbolized by his fool's garb and his apparent simplemindedness—to that of the consummate insider, who brings all the disparate elements of the plot together in a complex weave of kinship relationships. Parzival's hesitation on the occasion of his first visit to Munsalvaesche, in sum, not only has a psychological motivation; it also suggests his unreadiness to bring about the synthesis into which he must slowly mature. He is far from ready at that point to become king of the Grail.[16] Wolfram provides us with various markers by which we can measure Parzival's growth toward compassion and humility—the internalization of the true values of knighthood and Christianity. At each of his repeated encounters with such figures as Sigune, Jeschute, and Trevrizent his response is more mature.[17] In addition, Parzival's clothing—from his initial fool's garb to his glamorous knightly armor to his symbolic disrobing in Trevrizent's cave—reflects quite precisely the stages of his development.

At no point does Wolfram suggest that either of the two realms is defective or superior to the other.[18] (Wolfram's fictional world consists only of these two poles, church and state; the peasant estate is scarcely mentioned, much less the historically significant bourgeoisie in the incipient urban culture of the High Middle Ages. In addition, we hear nothing about the Church as an institution—only about religion as faith.) True, the realms of religion and knighthood as he first experiences them are imperfect. The primitive Christian community that Herzeloyde has created in the forest of Soltane lacks structure and depth; and Arthur's court, when Parzival first irrupts into it, displays signs of both arrogance and cruelty.[19] Moreover, the courtly society of Schastel Marveile under Clinschor's curse is as defective as Munsalvaesche under the stigma of Anfortas's wound. However, both are ultimately redeemed by heroes motivated by unsullied knighthood and pure religious compassion. If Wolfram regards a liberated Munsalvaesche under the kingship of Parzival as superior in any way to Arthur's court, then it is because Munsalvaesche now represents a knighthood enhanced by the values of Christian faith.[20] And if we now recall that Parzival's hesitation was caused by superficial practices of society that inhibited him from yielding to normal human impulses, then we might reasonably conclude that Wolfram's principal concern was for the dangers of an oversecularized knighthood that was losing all sense of its original religious values. (Gawan, the paragon of secular knighthood, disappears from the story with no further mention after book 15. There is no place for a simple knight, be he ever so pure, at Munsalvaesche.) But this observation brings us to concluding observations on the issues of *Parzival* as a reflection of Wolfram's own society.

FIN-DE-SIÈCLE CONCERNS

It is generally accepted that Wolfram wrote his *Parzival* during the first decade of the thirteenth century.[21] Of course we should not read it as a social or political allegory any more than we did in the cases of the *Aeneid* or the *Oresteia*—and certainly not as an attack on the church or state of Wolfram's own day. At the same time, Wolfram was no more able than Virgil or Aeschylus to escape the assumptions of his age. For instance, his epic romance displays a fascination with all three of the cultural realms that obsessed his contemporaries. The story of Gahmuret (bks. 1 and 2) and the appearance of Feirefiz (bk. 15)—as well as Wolfram's frequent references to his (spurious?) Arabic source and to oriental lore—suggest the current fascination with the East resulting from the Crusades and the recent discovery of Arabic learning. Wolfram's repeated allusions to episodes from the *Aeneid,* with which he was acquainted in the adaptation of Heinrich von Veldeke, adumbrate a second area of renewed contemporary interest: classical antiquity. It is likely, moreover, that he was generally acquainted with the medievalized version of the *Oresteia* as retold as a courtly episode in Benoît de Sainte-Maure's twelfth-century *Roman de Troie.* (While Wolfram could not have known Aeschylus's *Libation Bearers,* a striking parallel to Clytemnestra's nightmare of the destructive snake—derived no doubt from common folkloristic sources—is evident in Herzeloyde's terrifying dream, in which she gives birth to a serpent that tears her womb and a dragon that sucks at her breasts before flying away [104.10–12].)[22] The basic plot-lines, revolving around King Arthur and the quest for the Holy Grail, are based on Celtic myth and legend by way of Chrétien de Troyes and point to the third major source of cultural interest: the so-called *matière de Bretagne.* To this extent *Parzival* amounts to a cultural *summa* of early thirteenth-century Germany.

Scholars have spent a great deal of time and ingenuity analyzing the theological implications of *Parzival,* especially of Trevrizent's elaborations in book 9, and suggesting connections to medieval theology (notably Augustine and Bernard of Clairvaux), medieval mysticism, and the great heresies and lay movements of the period.[23] It has been argued that Wolfram was a pre-Reformation Protestant, a devout Catholic, a secret practitioner of Manichaean or other heresies, and a *Mensch* in the lofty sense of Enlightenment humanism. On a more general level, however, and with greater relevance to our specific focus, the counterpoint of Round Table and Grail also points to the continuing struggle between emperors and popes, which constituted the principal political issue leading from the twelfth to the thirteenth century.

The tension between the two institutions had been mounting for centuries, with the Church declaring the priority of the papacy in the western Roman Empire while the State insisted that the consecration of the popes and investiture of bishops was valid only if approved by the emperor and other temporal rulers. The controversy between spiritual and secular powers came to a preliminary head toward the end of the eleventh century in the so-called Investiture Contest. At that time Pope Gregory VII made the exorbitant demand that the Church should have full authority over the secular sovereigns. His demand was denounced by King Heinrich IV, who in turn was excommunicated by the pope. In the effort to save himself from deposition by the princes who sided with the pope, in 1077 Heinrich made his humiliating barefoot pilgrimage to Canossa in the northern Apennines to obtain release from the ban. The controversy was finally resolved at the Concordat of Worms in 1122, when Pope Calixtus II and Emperor Heinrich V divided the powers of investiture between Church and State.

During the following three decades the power of the German emperors was further eroded in favor of the papacy until 1152, when Friedrich Barbarossa was elected to the kingship. Friedrich had not sought the pope's approval, as was normally expected, but merely notified him. Eugenius II, needing the assistance of the new sovereign in order to maintain his own temporal power in Rome, gave way. His successors, however, notably Alexander III (1159–81), renewed the struggle, forcing Barbarossa, following his catastrophic defeat at Legnano in 1176, to kneel and acknowledge the spiritual supremacy of the Holy See. Alexander's immediate successors were unable to sustain this papal momentum, especially against the vigorous reign of Barbarossa's son, Heinrich VI (1189–96). They were followed, however, by one of the greatest medieval popes, Innocent III, whose ambition was to consolidate all power, both secular and temporal, under the Church—to be at once pope and emperor, *caput ecclesiae* and *caput mundi*. And precisely during the period when Wolfram was writing *Parzival* he seemed to be succeeding in his dream. He was confronted by a Germany without a strong ruler, a land divided for almost ten years by the rivalry between the elected king, Philipp of Swabia, and the so-called anti-king, Otto of Brunswick, who was elected by a minority of princes and supported by the pope. As a result, Wolfram's Germany was weakened by internal strife and still under the sway of papal imperialism.

It is difficult to look at *Parzival* and its tension between Court and Grail, between Arthur and Anfortas, without suspecting at least some reflection of the struggle between empire and papacy that dominated the age. If that is the case, then it is tempting to see in Parzival's reconciliation of the two realms an expression of Wolfram's hope that a similar resolution might be brought to the conflict causing so much turmoil and grief for his own contemporaries.

This same period witnessed another development with implications for *Parzival*: the first four Crusades (1096–99, 1147–49, 1189–92, and 1202–4), the last of which took place as Wolfram was writing. Leaving aside the military failures of the expeditions and the imperialistic goals only partially masked by religious propaganda, the Crusades fulfilled at least two important functions with regard to Wolfram's epic romance. They exposed the Christian West to an Arabic culture whose superiority in many respects had to be acknowledged, an aesthetic and scientific superiority frequently cited by Wolfram. And they created an order of knights who provided in many respects the model for the *templeise* of Munsalvaesche: the Knights Templar, a military order founded in 1119 to protect pilgrims to the Holy Land, who took an oath to forsake worldly chivalry and to live in chastity, obedience, and poverty.[24] This order, at least as an ideal, represented a reaction against the increasing secularization of the knighthood that concerned Wolfram—its liberation, as evident in King Arthur's knights of the Round Table, from any controlling religious authority.

We see, then, that Parzival's moment of hesitation, which is not quickly resolved like that of Aeneas and Orestes but initiates a period of more than four years of uncertainty and development, has essentially the same function as theirs. Keen observer of the human soul that he is, Wolfram has provided us with a perfectly adequate psychological motivation—Parzival's naive literal-mindedness and immature inability to reach moral decisions for himself and his unreadiness at that early point in his emotional and ethical development to become king of the Grail. But only a superficial reading would be content with that explanation. Parzival's hesitation symbolizes a larger conflict between the two great realms of being that constitute the fictional world of the epic romance—religion and knighthood, thought and action, *vita activa* and *vita contemplativa*. And these realms reflect, in turn, the conflict between Church and State, between pope and emperor, in Wolfram's own age. Parzival ultimately seeks to resolve that tension, rather than accepting one goal in preference to the other. And that idealizing effort, as impossible of realization as it may be in reality, puts Wolfram's great epic romance in the company of Virgil's *Aeneid* and Aeschylus's *Oresteia*.

4

Hamlet, or Anomy in Elsinor

HAMLET, AENEAS, ORESTES

The scene is unforgettable. The traveling players visiting Elsinore have just performed *The Murder of Gonzago,* and Hamlet has closely observed his uncle to see "if his occulted guilt / Do not itself unkennel in one speech" (3.2.5–6). The results are even more vivid and conclusive than anticipated by Hamlet, who hoped simply to see the king "blench" (2.2.626). At the fateful moment—as the murderer pours poison into Gonzago's ear—Claudius starts up from his seat in fright and rushes from the hall, crying for light. A short time later, as Hamlet is on his way to see his mother, he passes the room where Claudius, overcome suddenly by the consciousness of his "rank offence" and guilt, is kneeling at prayer. Drawing his sword, Hamlet thinks: "Now might I do it pat, now he is praying; / And now I'll do 't" (3.3.73–74). But even as he stealthily advances with his weapon in hand, he has second thoughts. For if he kills Claudius "in the purging of his soul," he will simply send him to heaven—an act that would be tantamount to "hire and salary, no revenge." He sheathes his sword and decides to wait for a more carnal moment "When he is drunk asleep, or in his rage, / Or in the

74

incestuous pleasure of his bed" so that "his soul may be as damn'd and black / As hell, whereto it goes."

At least for a century since A. C. Bradley's classic lectures on Shakespeare's tragedies this scene has been regarded by many as the "turning point" of the play.[1] In any case, the moment of hesitation is so striking that it invites comparison with two of the works that we have already considered. Both Aeneas and Orestes, as we saw, experience similar moments of hesitation, but for them the outcome is fatally different. That Shakespeare was familiar, at least in general outline, with the *Aeneid,* cannot be doubted. (Gawin Douglas's translation—the first into English—had been in print since 1553.) But there is more specific evidence. On the preceding day Hamlet had requested one of the players to recite a favorite speech of his: Aeneas's account of Pyrrhus's slaughter of Priam (based loosely here on a scene from *Dido Queen of Carthage* [1594] by Christopher Marlowe and Thomas Nashe [2.1.221–60]).[2] The lines, recited at length—indeed, "too long" according to Polonius—portray in gory detail how Pyrrhus, seeking vengeance for the death of his father Achilles, remorselessly kills the aged Trojan king, "mincing his limbs" with his sword (2.2.472–541). Hamlet makes it clear in his subsequent monologue, to which we shall return, that he wanted to hear the speech in order to whip up his own fury for vengeance.[3] While Shakespeare does not refer to Aeneas's later killing of Turnus, he clearly sees an anticipation of Hamlet's hesitation in the moment when Pyrrhus, having struck down Priam, pauses before dealing the fatal blow:

> for, lo! his sword,
> Which was declining on the milky head
> Of reverend Priam, seem'd i' the air to stick:
> So, as a painted tyrant, Pyrrhus stood,
> And like a neutral to his will and matter,
> Did nothing.
>
> (2.2.499–504)

Recent scholars have been more generous in their assessment of Shakespeare's knowledge of Latin in a curriculum centered around

Virgil. They point to the similarities in each case of the heroes' special relationship with their fathers, to the love affairs frustrated by the tension between *amor* and *fatum,* to the conflict between justice and revenge, and to the filial *pietas* that can be achieved only by an act of *impius furor.*[4]

Hamlet has also often been compared to Orestes, and recent evidence has made it increasingly likely that Shakespeare was acquainted with some version of the *Oresteia,* perhaps through one of the Latinized translations of the sixteenth century.[5] Certainly their situations are in many respects astonishingly similar.[6] Both have lost beloved fathers, who were great warriors and kings, to murderers who not only usurped their kingdoms but also married their queens. Both are young men—not mature heroes—who come from abroad (Phocis and Wittenberg) with the benefit of an outsider's point of view and accompanied by loyal friends (Pylades and Horatio). Both are incited to action by supernatural agents (Apollo's oracle as well as the conjured spirit of Agamemnon and the ghost of Hamlet's father). Both attempt in highly charged dialogues to shame their mothers for consorting with the murderers of their fathers. Both must disguise their feelings, and madness—genuine in Orestes and feigned in Hamlet—is central to their stories. Both experience considerable uncertainty before they are satisfied enough about the guilt to proceed to the punishment of the regicides. But there the similarity ends, for Orestes acts at the decisive moment. And while his actions, as well as those of Aeneas, save their societies, they have dire personal consequences for the heroes. Aeneas's slaying of Turnus decisively marks the defeat of the native Italian tribes and opens the way for the glorious Roman future prophesied by Anchises. But Aeneas himself dies only three years later and his reputation has suffered ever since in the state of ambiguity discussed earlier. Was the killing morally and politically justified and necessary, or was it merely an impulsive act of revenge? As for Orestes, he liberates Argos from the detested tyranny of Clytemnestra and Aegisthus, but he himself is immediately set upon by the horrid Furies and hounded off to Delphi and Athens.

Hamlet's case is quite different. Had he acted, then everything we have learned in the play about his popularity—he is "loved of the distracted multitude" (4.3.4)— suggests that his reasons for killing Claudius would have been accepted by the people and that he would quickly have been acclaimed the king of Denmark. (In act 4, scene 5, the rabble are fully prepared to declare Laertes king when Claudius is believed responsible for Polonius's death.) Moreover, unlike Orestes he has no reason to murder his mother, who, despite her adultery and incest, is innocent of her first husband's murder and probably ignorant of Claudius's role in it. Hamlet might easily have lived happily ever after, married to Ophelia, with Gertrud as dowager queen and Polonius if no longer lord chamberlain then as court jester, and surrounded by such loyal friends as Horatio and Laertes. (We recall that Clytemnestra futilely tried to persuade Orestes to spare her life and to live on with her in Argos.) Auden has even suggested that Hamlet, before the murder of his father, "was no hero, just an ordinary pleasant young man."[7] As matters turn out, however, Hamlet's failure to act triggers a sequence of deaths that might otherwise have been avoided: those of Polonius, Ophelia, Rosenkrantz and Guildenstern, Laertes, Claudius, Gertrud—and, of course, Hamlet himself.

THE PRELIMINARIES

It is important, in the light of our topic and the comparisons with Aeneas and Orestes, to make a careful distinction between the critical moment of *hesitation* almost precisely in the middle of *Hamlet* (act 3, scene 3) and the more general tactic of *delay* that characterizes Hamlet's behavior up to that point. Hamlet is no coward and no stranger to cold-blooded decisiveness and courageous action.[8] From various hints in the play (Ophelia's words at 3.1.159, for example) we are led to believe that the thirty-year-old has had at least some military experience, and in any case he is an accomplished swordsman. He strikes quickly and accurately when he hears Polonius's voice behind the arras. He leaps boldly onto the pirate ship which attacks his vessel on its way to England. He coolly sends the traitorous Rosencrantz and Guildenstern to their certain deaths in England. In their duel he scores the first two hits on Laertes, whose swordsmanship is renowned even in France. And he does not hesitate to plunge his sword into Claudius's chest when his uncle's treachery is publicly exposed. Why does such an otherwise brave, even impulsive man hesitate and delay?

Ever since Goethe's perceptive (if now controversial) analysis over two centuries ago, critics have often found it useful to ask themselves what sort of man Hamlet was up to the moment of his father's death.[9] At the age of thirty he has won the friendship of many—Horatio, Laertes, Rosencrantz and Guildenstern (even if the latter subsequently betray him)—and the love of Ophelia. A devout and admiring son, he nurtures a faithful and enduring affection for his father and, clad in "inky cloak" (1.2.77), mourns the paternal death—which he still does not know to have been murder—long after the other members of the court have put away their "nighted colour" (1.2.68). He displays a pronounced aesthetic sense, enjoying theatrical performances and memorizing passages of favorite plays. An able courtier, he can both detect dissemblance in others and deceive in return, and he moves resourcefully amid the dangers of the Danish court. Blessed with a quick wit and an enviable command of logic and rhetoric, he is not reluctant to exhibit a sharp tongue even to the king. He converses easily not just with other courtiers but also with soldiers on the ramparts and with the gravediggers in the churchyard. Above all he has benefited from his studies at Wittenberg. (Whether those studies took place in the immediate past or some years earlier remains a matter of scholarly dispute.) In sum, he has rightfully been called an "ideal Renaissance nobleman,"[10] aspiring to the synthesis of soldier and scholar, of Mars and Mercury, which he saw exemplified by his father (3.4.57–58).[11] Unlike Aeneas, Orestes, and Parzival, Hamlet is the first of our hesitant heroes who can properly be called an intellectual.

As a true son of his age, moreover, he believes in the "god-like reason" invested in man (4.4.38) and the "discourse of reason" lacking in beasts (1.2.150). "What a piece of work is a man," he exclaims; "how noble in reason! how infinite in faculty" (2.2.314–15). He possesses the capacity for easy generalization and universalization, and he makes sophisticated use of paradox, syllogism, and other devices of Renaissance logic to question the world around him, which he no longer takes for granted with medieval absoluteness. (The comic *reductio ad absurdum* of Hamlet's dialectical thinking is evident in the gravedigger's ruminations.) And he has an almost unlimited belief in the power of language, which he wields as effectively as daggers (3.2.414) against anyone who comes within range. Accordingly he is beset by perfectly reasonable doubts when he encounters what purports to be the ghost of his father. It would have been utterly out of character for this Renaissance scholar, this critical mind trained at the Protestant university of Wittenberg, this "personification of doubtfulness,"[12] to accept immediately and without reservation the words of such a medieval phenomenon as a ghost from an obviously Catholic purgatory.[13] It is difficult, therefore, to go along with the view that Hamlet, when first we meet him, is little more than a "distracted undergraduate."[14] All his responses appear to be those not of an untried youth but of a mature man of thirty whose rational beliefs, honed by the finest contemporary education, are being tested.[15] The apparition of the ghost plunges him into an intellectual chaos and requires him for the first time to question his hitherto stable world order—that "collapse of the subjective world of the tragic hero" which is the hallmark of Shakespeare's mature tragedies.[16]

It has often been remarked, as has almost everything else in this much-expounded work, that this play about questions and doubts begins with a question: that, indeed, the interrogative is the principal mode of the first scene—"Who's there?"—as well as the entire drama—"To be, or not to be: that is the question."[17] But the questions in the play belong logically to a particular category: they represent—at least initially—no generalized doubt regarding any and all meaning but, in the classic sense, a dilemma, a *dubitatio,* a choice between alternatives, a Kierkegaardian "either/or." This dialectical dualism, this bipolar and binary cast of thought, is evident rhetorically in the frequent reduplications and antitheses (Polonius's advice) and doublings—two Hamlets, two Fortinbras (father and son), Rosencrantz and Guildenstern—which "charge the air with overtones of wavering and indecision."[18]

The ghost that stalks the ramparts of Elsinore at midnight represents, then, an irruption of the irrational into Hamlet's hitherto rational world—an irruption that his friend and fellow student Horatio also initially regards as "fantasy" (1.1.23).[19] Accordingly his instinct is to question, doubt, and challenge the phenomenon, and even two months later he still wonders if the "damned ghost" was merely a product of his foul imagination (3.2.87–88). True, he is dismayed by his father's recent death (two months earlier), disgusted by his mother's even more recent and incestuous marriage to an uncle he detests (one month earlier), and appalled at the scandalous behavior of the court, which has already made Denmark the laughing stock of other nations.[20] For this reason, when his friend Laertes goes back to Paris after the funeral and wedding, Hamlet contemplates a return (after a longer or shorter absence) to Wittenberg—not simply to pursue the studies he enjoys, but mainly to remove himself from a situation he finds almost intolerable. Up to this point, however, despite the suspicions of his "prophetic soul" (1.5.40) he has had no compelling reason to believe that his father's death was anything but normal. So he reluctantly agrees—out of courtesy for his mother, at least token respect for the new king, and perhaps in the hope of accomplishing some good—to remain at Elsinore.

When Horatio then reports the wonder he witnessed the previous night on the ramparts, Hamlet through his many questions—no fewer than eleven!— betrays his considerable skepticism. But he is curious enough to want to share the watch that same night in case the ghost should manifest itself again and, assuming his father's form, speak to him. When the ghost does indeed appear, Hamlet appeals to the "angels and ministers of grace" for their protection and then interrogates the apparition with typically dichotomous rhetoric:

> Be thou a spirit of health or goblin damn'd,
> Bring with thee airs from heaven or blasts from hell,
> Be thy intents wicked or charitable,
> Thou comest in such a questionable shape
> That I will speak to thee.
>
> (1.4.40–44)

First of all, he wants to know why the ghost has broken all the laws of nature by leaving its sepulchre to "revisit the glimpses of the moon," forcing him and other poor fools of nature "So horridly to shake our disposition / With thoughts beyond the reaches of our souls" (1.4.555–56). These words give voice to the reason that doubts so irrational a phenomenon. When Hamlet is exhorted to follow the specter to a more remote part of the ramparts, Horatio warns that it "might deprive your sovereignty of reason / And draw you into madness" (1.4.73–74).

The ghost informs Hamlet that it is indeed his father's spirit, condemned for a time to purgatory, which it is forbidden to describe, until his sins are burnt away and purged. Then, for the first time, he introduces the term "murder"—"most foul, strange and unnatural" (1.5.28)—to characterize his death. In his immediate emotional reaction Hamlet speaks of revenge—but still only after his intellect *knows* more specific details.

> Haste me to know't, that I, with wings as swift
> As meditation or the thoughts of love,
> May sweep to my revenge.
>   (1.5.30–31)

The ghost reports that his death, falsely attributed to a serpent's sting, actually resulted from poison poured into his ear by his brother Claudius. He also tells Hamlet that even before his death Gertrude was involved adulterously with Claudius; yet he urges his son not to punish his mother, but to "leave her to heaven" and to her own guilty conscience. At that, the specter departs, leaving Hamlet to thoughts of vengeance. But he swears his friends to silence about the night's doings—an oath that suggests his own uncertainty. His words indicate a certain tension in his mind between what he seems to have seen and everything he has previously known: "There are more things in heaven and earth, Horatio, / Than are dreamt of in your philosophy" (1.5.166–67)—a philosophy, after all, that Hamlet had also studied and learned at Wittenberg. When he complains in his closing words of act 1 that "The time is out of joint" and regrets "That ever I was born to set it right" we surely do not go astray if we hear in that lament, beyond its obvious local meaning, a reference to the metaphysical uncertainty and doubt brought into his rational world by the apparition of a ghost. Certainly we can find more than ample reason to justify his delay.[21] A trained mind does not lapse from rationality into a belief in the irrational from one moment to the next.

HAMLET'S "ANTIC DISPOSITION"

Two months pass (between acts 1 and 2) before we see Hamlet again, and in the intervening period he has lapsed as planned into an "antic disposition" (1.5.172), drifting around Elsinore with "his stockings foul'd, / Ungarter'd, and down-gyved to his ancle" (2.1.79–80)—a transformation causing some at court to believe that he has gone mad from his love of Ophelia but one that prompts the more suspicious Claudius to send for Hamlet's friends Rosencrantz and Guildenstern to test his disposition. Hamlet's quick decision shortly after his encounter with the ghost to feign madness betrays a highly rational and reasonable mind at work. It suggests, first, a lingering doubt regarding the meaning of the apparition: did it in truth represent the voice of his murdered father? or was it a phantom sent to delude him—a projection of his own tormented mind and desire to punish his mother and uncle? And it suggests, in addition, a reasonable assessment of the danger to him should he in fact determine the truth of the ghost's utterance and decide to act on it in revenge. After all, Claudius is the king and has all the king's power at his disposal and bodyguards surrounding him. So Hamlet's delay and feigned madness mark the calculated decision of a reasonable man. This appears to be consistent with the conclusion reached by Hegel in his *Aesthetics,* where the ghost is presented as "an objective form of Hamlet's inner premonition" and Hamlet's hesitation is understood as a manifestation of doubts he must overcome through his own efforts before he can put aside his "inner harmony" and act.[22]

At the same time, this necessary tactic of delay while he waits for proof and opportunity does not sit well with a man accustomed to action. When he sees the player's tears for Hecuba following his recitation, he is moved to shame: "What would he do, / Had he the

motive and the cue for passion / That I have?" (2.2.586–88). Even
his intelligence and reason shame Hamlet because he, "Prompted
to my revenge by heaven and hell, / Must, like a whore, unpack my
heart with words" (2.2.613–14). Yet his rational mind requires certainty. So he decides upon the device of the play, *The Murder of Gonzago,* whose plot parallels the circumstances of the murder as
recounted by his father's ghost. He still worries that "The spirit that
I have seen / May be the devil: and the devil hath power / To assume a pleasing shape." Indeed, the devil may have exploited Hamlet's own emotions, "my weakness and my melancholy," to mislead,
confuse, and damn him.

Rosencrantz and Guildenstern are not clever enough to unmask
Hamlet, who immediately senses their mission. In his famous monologue, however, he betrays his own lingering doubts. The first two-
thirds of the often-quoted speech (3.1.56–89) amount to a meditation
on the *vita activa* versus the *vita contemplativa,* which quickly gives way
in turn to reflections on suicide—a freely chosen death that would liberate us from all "the whips and scorns of time." It is again uncertainty,
uncertainty regarding the afterlife, that gives him pause: "the dread of
something after death," of dreams that might torment us even in
death.

> Thus conscience does make cowards of us all;
> And thus the native hue of resolution
> Is sicklied o'er with the pale cast of thought,
> And enterprises of great pitch and moment
> With this regard their currents turn awry,
> And lose the name of action.

Let us remind ourselves that Hamlet is using the vocable "conscience" in the older sense that still involved the primary meaning
of "consciousness":[23] that is, of intellectual consideration as well as
moral awareness. (Hamlet locates his sufferings, after all, in his
"mind" and is worried about ills "that we *know* not of" [my italics].)
This is not to deny any moral qualms on his part; but the lines un-
derscore his lingering intellectual doubts.

It is these doubts that he seeks to allay as he watches Claudius dur-

ing the players' performance of *The Murder of Gonzago*. And that reaction is so clear that Hamlet is finally prepared to "take the ghost's
word for a thousand pound" (3.2.297–98). But as he follows his
mother's invitation to call upon her in her chamber he is still resolved to be "cruel, not unnatural: / I will speak daggers to her, but
use none" (3.2.413–14). It is in such a mood that he catches Claudius at prayer.

We can now recapitulate. Hamlet's words, as he approaches Claudius with the intent to kill and then backs away again, reveal his conscious thoughts, but not all the unconscious ones, the inhibitions
that undermine his resolve. His immediate justification, in fact, is a
bit lame, for Hamlet has hitherto given little indication of the kind
of profound religious concern that would persuade us that his hesitation out of regard for heaven and hell is heartfelt.[24] To be sure,
it is superficially plausible and fits the expected moral criteria of the
age. But everything that has preceded, as well as much that follows,
leads us to believe that his resolution has been shaken by intellectual doubts—by his "conscience" in the Renaissance sense of the
word. One brief moment, one unexpected opportunity cannot
overcome the habit of delay and consideration produced by the
skepticism, the philosophical doubts, of his mind. This conclusion
is supported by his next great soliloquy just before his departure for
England (4.4.32–66). There it is still reason distinguishing rational man from the rest of creation that concerns him. The key words
are still intellectual: "reason," "thinking," "thought," "wisdom," and
"cause."

> What is a man,
> If his chief good and market of his time
> Be but to sleep and feed? a beast, no more.
> Sure, he that made us with such large discourse,
> Looking before and after, gave us not
> That capability and god-like reason
> To fust in us unused. Now, whether it be
> Bestial oblivion, or some craven scruple
> Of thinking too precisely on the event,
> A thought which, quarter'd, hath but one part wisdom
> And ever three parts coward, I do not know

Why yet I live to say 'This thing's to do;'
Sith I have cause and will and strength and means
To do't.

After the turning point marked by Hamlet's hesitation and despite several great scenes, the dénouement of the tragedy follows almost routinely. Hamlet stabs the eavesdropping Polonius behind
the arras. Shipped off to England, he outwits Rosencrantz and
Guildenstern, sending them to their own deaths and escaping with
the help of the pirates. When a raging Laertes returns from France
to find his father dead and his sister gone mad and drowned,
Claudius shrewdly turns all this fury against Hamlet. When Hamlet
returns to Elsinore, resolved now to destroy the man who has killed
his father and whored his mother, his conversations with the gravedigger and with Horatio show us a reasonable man in full control
of his faculties. To be sure, overcome by one of his sudden impulses
to action he brawls with Laertes in Ophelia's grave but then readily
makes peace with him. As a result, he does not suspect chicanery
when Claudius invites him to swordplay for a wager with Laertes. In
the ensuing mêlée with poisoned rapiers and goblets all the princi-
pals are killed: Laertes, Claudius, Gertrude, and Hamlet. Fortinbras
arrives to claim the kingdom of Denmark for Norway and arranges
a burial with military honors for Hamlet, while Horatio promises to
tell the full and true story—which, at this point, the audience already knows.

THE ROTTEN STATE

The apparition of the ghost precipitates the confusion and anguish
in Hamlet's mind, which he conceals on a superficial level by the
appearance of madness. The feigned madness, however, is a brilliant image for the true illness that consumes Hamlet: his frantic attempt to come to grips with the intrusion of the irrational into the
rational world that defies all the known laws of nature—when "hell
itself breathes out / Contagion to this world" (3.2.407–08). He
may well use the excuse of his "diseased wit" to avoid giving "whole-

some answers" (3.2.333–34); but his "distemper," which is re-marked upon by at least three different people (3.2.312 and 350; 3.4.123), is genuine to the extent that it is a symptom of his intel-lectual quandary. And Hamlet's distemper, in turn, is a microcos-mic manifestation of the disease that afflicts the greater world of the play.[25]

When Horatio first glimpses the ghost, he immediately suspects that "This bodes some strange eruption to our state" (1.1.69). And when the apparition summons Hamlet to a private conference, Marcellus concludes that "Something is rotten in the state of Den-mark" (1.4.90). Claudius knows that Fortinbras of Norway is en-couraged in his demands on Denmark because he thinks "Our state to be disjoint and out of frame" (1.2.20), and Hamlet remarks in serious jest that "Denmark's a prison" (2.2.249).

But the affliction has come from within. After Hamlet has killed Polonius, Claudius regrets that he has allowed so much freedom of movement to a man who represents a threat to the public. He ra-tionalizes his inaction by his affection for Hamlet.

> We would not understand what was most fit;
> But, like the owner of a foul disease,
> To keep it from divulging, let it feed
> Even on the pith of life.
>
> (4.1.20–23)

Claudius's words, however, represent an accurate diagnosis of his own reign, which was won by murder—a deed known to the audi-ence and Hamlet but still "undivulged" to the court, the people, and even Gertrude, and, like a festering disease, feeding on its new power. Gertrude, blinded by the sexual passion that led her into adultery with Claudius while her husband was still alive, lives mind-lessly, as Hamlet puts it, "In the rank sweat of an enseamed bed, / Stew'd in corruption, honeying and making love / Over the nasty sty" (3.4.93–95). The court has likewise been infected by the dis-ease, for Claudius is easily able to exploit senior counselors such as Polonius, to corrupt the trust of Hamlet's one-time friends, Rosen-crantz and Guildenstern, and to redirect the fury of Laertes. The

people, too, Claudius realizes, are "muddied, / Thick and unwholesome in their thoughts and whispers" (4.5.81–82).

The situation at Elsinore is characterized by a decline and fall exemplified by Ophelia's rapid transformation from health through
madness to death. Hamlet repeatedly points out to his mother that
her second marriage marked the shift from "Hyperion to a satyr"
(1.2.140) and "like a mildew'd ear, / Blasting his wholesome
brother" (3.4.64–65). The kingdom once governed by a king who
defeated "ambitious Norway" and "smote the sledded Polacks on
the ice" (1.1.61–63) is now ruled by a man who "takes his rouse, /
Keeps wassail, and the swaggering up-spring reels" as he gulps down
Rhine wine. Denmark is ridiculed abroad as the nation of drunk-
ards and swine. This behavior, as Hamlet laments, "takes / From
our achievements, though perform'd at height, / The pith and
marrow of our attribute" (1.4.20–22). As the action begins, Denmark is like a patient in the early stages of a particularly malignant
cancer: apparently healthy on the outside, with a new king and a re-
married queen and jolly revels, but decaying rapidly from the inside
until virtually its entire nobility lies dead on the floor, poisoned
from within. Shakespeare even hints gloomily that circumstances
will not change much for the better once the disease has been seemingly eradicated by the multiple deaths. The new ruler Fortinbras,
for all his noble words at the end, has already shown himself to be
infected by the "impostume of much wealth and peace" (4.4.27)
and willing, for the sheer glory, to sacrifice two thousand men and
twenty thousand ducats for a worthless strip of land in Poland. As
Georg Lukács observed, "At the end of each of Shakespeare's great
tragedies a whole world collapses, and we find ourselves at the dawn
of an entirely new epoch."[26]

It is fitting, as scholars have noted, that the favored means of
death in this corrupt body politic is poison.[27] The "leprous distil-
ment" that Claudius pours into the elder Hamlet's ear quickly con-
taminates his "thin and wholesome blood" and covers his smooth
body with a "vile and loathsome crust" (1.5.63–73). The unction
bought from a quack, with which Laertes anoints the tip of his
rapier, is so toxic that not even the most potent antidote can save
from death anyone scratched by it (4.7.141–49). As a precaution,

should Hamlet escape Laertes' venomed rapier, Claudius prepares a chalice with "a poison temper'd by himself" (5.2.339)—the poison by which Gertrude subsequently dies. So obsessed is Claudius with poisons that the idea even colors his language. Thus he tells Laertes that the report of Laertes' skillful swordsmanship did "envenom" Hamlet with his envy (4.7.104).

The stealth of poison in the body is matched by the secrecy and deception in a courtly society where everyone lies to everyone else.[28] Claudius has lied to his wife about the murder of her first husband. Polonius sends Reynaldo to Paris to spy on his son, Laertes, and to gather information by falsehoods. Claudius and Polonius hide behind the arras to spy on Hamlet and Ophelia, and Polonius conceals himself to eavesdrop on Hamlet and Gertrude. Rosencrantz and Guildenstern attempt to deceive Hamlet, first about the reasons for their return from Wittenberg and then about their mission to England. Claudius lies to Laertes in order to focus the latter's rage on Hamlet. Claudius and Laertes deceive Hamlet about the swordplay. Hamlet's "madness" is an act of deception. Small wonder that a young woman as innocent and unsophisticated as Ophelia goes mad in a world like this!

TIME OUT OF JOINT

The tale of Hamlet goes back beyond the early thirteenth-century *Gesta Danorum* of Saxo Grammaticus into the mists of the Germanic past. Gilbert Murray has suggested that its roots can be traced back to an *Urmythos* revolving around the king of the Golden Bough, which also underlies the legend of Orestes and therefore relates the two.[29] If his assumption is correct, then it would also link those two legends to that of Parzival, whose origins as quester for the Holy Grail have been sought in the same source.[30]

Shakespeare's *Hamlet,* however, is firmly located in a contemporary Renaissance world characterized by English-style traveling players, by *Bildungsreisen* to Paris, by Machiavellian politics, by a Protestant university in Wittenberg, and by Medicean poison as the weapon of choice. These frequent allusions to England, France,

Germany, Italy, and the world at large alert us to the fact that Hamlet reflects not only the political situation of his native Denmark but the intellectual thought of the Renaissance world of his time. It has been often remarked that "Hamlet's downfall enacts the epistemological anxiety of the age."[31] His moment of hesitation in the middle of the action can now be seen as a point of balance not merely between a theological antithesis of heaven and hell, but as the moment at which his refuge into the acquired and carefully maintained polarities of dialectics gives way to a more generalized anxiety regarding truth and the nature of reality altogether. Here we find ourselves in a world quite different from that of the earlier hesitant heroes, all of whom were torn between two opposing systems of belief. In the case of Aeneas and Orestes, as we saw, the ancient ideology of blood vengeance came into conflict, on the one hand, with the prophesied ideal of a peaceful Roman rule and, on the other, with the new Athenian system of human law and justice. Parzival, by analogy, found himself confused by the divergent claims of knighthood and religion, of church and state. Hamlet, in contrast to all three, moves beyond those binary opposites into a world where *all* existing systems and beliefs are called into question, including family loyalty, friendship, love, religious belief, and political conviction.

It is by now a commonplace of Shakespeare criticism that Hamlet's predicament—to avoid the polarism implied by the term "dilemma"—is another manifestation of a broader Renaissance skepticism expressed by such representative figures as John Donne, Montaigne, Erasmus, and Machiavelli.[32] Donne's *First Anniversary* (1611), for instance, takes the death of a fifteen-year-old girl as an occasion to analyze "The Anatomy of the World," which according to the conceit of the poem, has been deeply wounded by that death.[33] This conceit produces imagery that is astonishing in its similarity to that of *Hamlet*. To establish the theme, the world is apostrophized:

> So thou, sicke world, mistak'st thy selfe to bee
> Well, when alas, thou'rt in a Letargee.
> (23–24)

Elizabeth Drury's premature death, however, "hath taught us dearely, that thou art / Corrupt and mortall in thy purest part" (61–62). These reflections lead Donne to the gloomy conclusion that there is no health but, at best, "a neutralitee" (92) in the world.

> And can there be worse sicknesse, then to know
> That we are never well, nor can be so?
> (93–94)

Soon enough the familiar images of generational decay and social disjointedness appear.

> mankind decayes so soone,
> We're scarse our Fathers shadowes cast at noone.
> (143–44)

> Then, as mankinde, so is the worlds whole frame
> Quite out of joynt, almost created lame.
> (191–92)

And why? Because "new Philosophy cals all in doubt" (205). As a result, the former comforting systems of thought and belief have disappeared in a confusion of relativism.

> 'Tis all in pieces, all cohaerence gone;
> All just supply, and all Relation.
> (213–14)

Moreover, the sickness of the world is not specific and confined, but "rotten at the hart" (242) and consumed by infections and fevers that poison us.

> Corruptions in our braines, or in our harts,
> Poysoning the fountaines, whence our actions spring,
> Endanger us.
> (330–32)

Elizabeth Drury, the poet concludes, having celebrated the true birth of her soul through death, is well rid of this corrupt world.

The "new Philosophy" that calls everything into doubt is most frequently identified with Montaigne's radical skepticism as summed up cogently toward the end of the sixteenth century in the words "Que sçay-je?" that, as he tells us in his long *Apologie de Raimond Sebond* (bk. 2, chap. 12 of his *Essais*), he has adopted as the motto for his escutcheon. In examples drawn from every area of human thought—theology, ethics, natural science, and human psychology—Montaigne demonstrates the extent of human ignorance and the inability of the human mind to know anything with certainty. Since we are incapable of understanding either the macrocosmos of the universe or the microcosmos of man, we should suspend all absolute statements, all judgments, and confine ourselves to asking: "What do I know?"

While the epistemological controversies are frequently adduced in discussions of Shakespeare's world, other factors may also play a role in *Hamlet*. Religious strife—notably the struggle between rulers and clergy that characterized Wolfram's Germany—was also very much alive in England during the thirteenth, fourteenth, and fifteenth centuries, as power swayed back and forth between the kings and the popes and as various anticlerical movements sought to lodge all temporal power with the laity. In the early sixteenth century Henry VIII initially took a stand against Martin Luther and supported papal authority, but subsequently altered his position when the pope objected to his divorce from Catherine of Aragon. In consequence he established royal supremacy over the Church in England, prohibiting further payments to Rome, and named himself "Supreme Head in earth of the Church of England." In 1535 Thomas More was beheaded for objecting to his policies, and Thomas Cromwell as vicar-general began the ruthless inspection of monasteries, which soon led to their dissolution. German proselytizers for the Reformation were welcomed in England, and by 1549 the first Book of Common Prayer incorporated pronounced Lutheran ideas. Although Mary I later rejected much of Henry's ecclesiastical legislation, reestablished relations with Rome, and revived the heresy laws, Elizabeth I on her ascent to the throne in 1558 so firmly restored the authority of the crown that, in 1570, she was excommunicated by Pius V. During her reign citizens were punished for attending mass, and the Jesuits who came to England were treated as traitors and often executed. Recognizing the political value of the Church of England, she insisted on conformity and opposed such movements as Separatism and Puritanism.

I have outlined this familiar history in order to highlight the religious situation in England at the time of Elizabeth's death in 1603— at the precise time that Shakespeare was writing *Hamlet*. Quite apart from the much-discussed issue of purgatory—whether or not Shakespeare implied by his references any position in the debate between Catholicism and the Church of England, which officially denied its existence—,[34] it is clear that religious controversy and uncertainty added an existential element to the general epistemological anxieties of the period. And here I agree with the commonsense view that "the tension between issues in Shakespearean tragedy is more important than the issues themselves."[35] The underlying religious tension is summoned up effectively, if vaguely, by the ghost, by mention of purgatory, by the references to Wittenberg, by Claudius at prayer, and other allusions.

At least as important in the public consciousness as the continuing religious controversy—because it potentially affected every citizen in his or her daily life—was the fierce conflict in the legal world between the various courts of common law and the Court of Chancery, a conflict that reached its peak in the first decade of the sixteenth century before being resolved in 1616 by James I.[36] The tension had existed ever since 1330, when Edward III, over the objections of the common-law judges, formally established a Court of Chancery in which his chancellor could hear cases that the other judges refused to admit. As a result, two wholly independent systems of jurisprudence existed side by side in English law: common-law courts for cases involving property and the equity courts on behalf of persons. The chancellors, always ecclesiastics until the Reformation, were traditionally guided not by the letter or even the principles of the existing common law but by the doctrines of Christianity. It was through their agency that the essentially religious notion of equity or mercy (*misericordia*) was introduced into English legal thought—an issue discussed centrally in such widely consulted sixteenth-century handbooks as Christopher St. German's *Doctor and Student* (1523). It is not going too far to propose that Hamlet's deliberations as he watches Claudius at prayer are affected by considerations of this sort.

The presence of courts of equity in which strict law was tempered by mercy produced tensions. Many people who sought greater predictability in the law felt that Chancery was fickle and unreliable because it had no standards more constant than the chancellor's character or whim. The conflict between these various courts in the decades immediately before its resolution was the leading issue in legal justice in England and produced an atmosphere of uncertainty that finds its counterpart in the "rotten state" of Denmark.

The conflict is clearly evident in William Lambarde's *Archeion, or, A Discourse upon the High Courts of Iustice in England,* which was long a standard authority.[37] (Although the work was first published in 1635, it was written before 1591, widely copied, circulated, and discussed among Lambarde's colleagues at Lincoln's Inn, and exerted its influence on the courts of the realm decades before its first publication.) Lambarde justifies the need for the Chancery Court of Equity by referring to Aristotle. "For *written Lawes* must needs bee made in a generalitie, and grounded upon that which happeneth for the most part, because no wisedome of man can fore-see every thing in particularitie, which Experience and Time doth beget" (69). But Lambarde, who displays a healthy fear of social chaos, repeatedly stresses the importance of seeking a "golden mediocrity" between the majesty of the king and the authority of the common-law courts. The plaintiff requires the security of knowing where to take his complaint and needs certainty of knowing the law according to which his case will be adjudicated. Otherwise a state of legal anarchy prevails. "Shall the *King* and his *Councell* open a Court for all sorts of *Pleas* that be determinable by the course of *Common Law*? that were to set an *Anomy,* and to bring disorder, doubt, and incertaintie overall" (120).

Lambarde's *Archeion* provides the first documented use of the word "anomy" in English, but the term enjoyed a notable vogue in Renaissance England, also in theological circles, where the biblical

Greek vocable translated as *iniquitas* or "lawlessness" is *anomia*. Shakespeare was almost certainly personally acquainted with Lambarde, and there is good reason to assume that he was familiar with *Archeion;* we know that he had in his library Lambarde's earlier work *Archaionomia* (1568). Lambarde's great tract reflects the mood of the 1590s, the period of social upheaval and civil disorder following the defeat of the Armada in 1588. It was during these years that the conflict between the courts of common law and equity reached its greatest intensity. During the reign of Elizabeth "hundreds of cases were recorded in which one litigant had a *judgment* in his favor and the other litigant had a *decree* in his favor, in the same controversy."[38] In this confusion of courts, litigants often did not know where to turn. This is precisely the legal, social, and spiritual situation that Lambarde called "anomy"—a situation where norms have disappeared, where behavior has become unpredictable, where the law itself has become questionable.

"Anomy"—a term that since Émile Durkheim's classic work *Suicide* (1897) has entered our modern vocabulary to designate a sense of alienation from a society perceived as disrupted and uncertain and often coupled with antisocial behavior—therefore is precisely the word we need to describe the situation into which Hamlet is plunged by the apparition of the ghost at Elsinore.[39] The general mood of anomy is established in the very first scene, where Horatio and the two officers, standing on the ramparts in the (surely symbolic) dark, are amazed by the specter that stalks past them without speaking. The sense is heightened the next night when Hamlet speaks to the ghost, whose existence violates all the known laws of reason and nature.[40] His anomy accounts for the antisocial behavior of the feigned "madness" in which he veils himself. But it also underlies Ophelia's descent into true madness as well as Gertrude's carnal excesses. Above all, it lies behind Hamlet's apathy, Donne's "Letargee," and the delay that precedes the moment of hesitation. And the mood is communicated by a poetry that is as mysteriously compressed as any of the language we have seen in the *Aeneid*, the *Oresteia,* or *Parzival.*

Hamlet's moment of hesitation, in sum, exposes not just the conscious religious concerns that motivate him but more generally the epistemological anxieties of his age and the anomy stifling the world of Elsinore. For this reason, Hamlet longs not merely to obtain vengeance, but also to establish order in a decaying world.

> The time is out of joint: O cursed spite,
> That ever I was born to set it right!
>   (1.5.189–90)

5

Wallenstein, or Evasions in Bohemia

Wilhelm von Humboldt was reminded of the *Oresteia*. "You have made Wallenstein's family into a House of the Atrides," he wrote to his friend Friedrich Schiller, "where Fate resides, where the inhabitants are driven out; but where the observer tarries long and gladly in the desolated site."[1] Coleridge promptly translated two parts of Schiller's *Wallenstein* into English (1800), and Benjamin Constant condensed the entire work into a French classical tragedy in rhymed alexandrines (*Wallstein*, 1809). Madame de Staël pronounced it "the most national tragedy" ("la tragédie la plus nationale") ever produced on the German stage, a work marked by the beauty of its verse and the grandeur of its subject—one that entitled Germany to claim it had a new Shakespeare.[2] Thomas Carlyle raved that it "may safely be rated as the greatest dramatic work of which that century can boast"[3]—including France and England. Goethe told Johann Peter Eckermann in one of their conversations (23 July 1827) that *Wallenstein* is such a magnificent work "that of its kind nothing similar will occur a second time." Thomas Mann published an early short story ("Schwere Stunde," 1905; "A Weary Hour") about Schiller's discouragement as he was writing the drama, and later he wrote an appreciation of the play—a work of "European vision, universal compass"—which was subsequently incorporated into his lengthy *Essay on Schiller* (1955).[4] Still today *Wallenstein* is regarded by Germans—literary scholars and theatergoers alike—as perhaps the finest German tragedy and certainly as the greatest political drama.[5] Yet it is probably safe to say that few people in the Anglo-American world who claim to be literarily cultivated have ever seen or read Schiller's masterpiece, which, coming between the Sturm-und-Drang plays of his youth (*The Robbers, Don Carlos*) and the classical drams of his maturity (*Maria Stuart, Wilhelm Tell*), was the first fruit of his historical and philosophical studies of the 1790s (*On the Aesthetic Education of Man*). As Stephen Spender observed in 1959 at the bicentenary of the poet's birth, "For a long time Schiller's reputation outside Germany has been under several clouds," including "the English feeling that he is a kind of unsuccessful would-be Shakespeare."[6]

The *Wallenstein* trilogy has often been compared by its admirers since Humboldt and Mme de Staël to both classical Greek drama and Shakespeare. But the references to antiquity usually focus on Sophocles and Euripides; critics who invoke Aeschylus often go no further than Agamemnon as the hero who, like Wallenstein, walks unsuspectingly to his death on a red carpet.[7] The comparisons to Shakespeare rarely extend beyond *Richard III* and *Macbeth*.[8] For the purposes of our topic, however, the analogy to the *Aeneid,* the *Oresteia,* and especially to *Hamlet* will be more fruitful.

Schiller was well acquainted with all three works. He first became infatuated with the *Aeneid* as a student and later translated passages from books 2, 4, and 6 (of which only the first was published). Ten years before the completion of *Wallenstein* (1799) he was negotiating with the publisher Cotta to issue a German library of Greek tragedies after the model of Pierre Brumoy's *Théâtre des Grecs* (1749) and, in that connection, was working on an uncompleted) translation of *Agamemnon,* which he called "one of the most beautiful plays that ever emerged from a poet's mind."[9] During the most intensive phase of composition (1796–98) he was studying the entire corpus of Greek tragedy (which, unlike many of his contemporaries, he read not in the original but in French or German translation). As for Shakespeare, whose works Schiller knew in C. M. Wieland's prose translations, during those same years Schiller was engaged with Goethe in an intensive critical correspondence regarding his friend's novel *Wilhelm Meisters Lehrjahre* (1795–96; *Wilhelm Meister's Apprenticeship*), which includes extended discussions of *Hamlet* as well as the description of a performance of the play.[10] George Steiner has suggested that Schiller's "most significant debt [to Shakespeare] lies in the handling of the crowd,"[11] and Schiller's most recent biographer, among others, has pointed to the similar functions of Lady Macbeth and Wallenstein's sister in egging on their men to action.[12] For the pattern of delay followed by hesitation, which characterizes the hero's behavior, however, Wallenstein's true models are Orestes and Hamlet.

THE BACKGROUND

Schiller's vast "dramatic poem" (*dramatisches Gedicht* according to its generic subtitle) with its more than 7,500 lines is almost twice as long as *Hamlet* or the entire *Oresteia*.[13] At Goethe's urging and out of theatrical necessity, Schiller divided the work for performance into three parts, which are usually presented separately: *Wallensteins Lager* (*Wallenstein's Camp*), *Die Piccolomini* (*The Piccolominis*), and *Wallensteins Tod* (*Wallenstein's Death*). But Schiller intended it as an integral whole, and it is usually discussed as such. Indeed, it is perhaps best considered as a prologue (*Wallenstein's Camp*) followed by a ten-act drama. Many readers have agreed with George Steiner that, taken as a whole, it is "a play that is most vividly present when it is read."[14]

The play is based on an important episode from the Thirty Years' War (1618–48).[15] For decades—indeed, for the century since the Reformation—there had been tensions in the Holy Roman Empire between Catholics and Protestants, represented later by the imperial forces of the Catholic League and the princes of the Protestant Union. Under an imperial dispensation the kingdom of Bohemia enjoyed religious freedom, but in 1618 increasing Catholic pressure from Vienna precipitated an uprising by Protestant citizens. The Protestant Union, sending forces to support the revolt, defeated the imperial armies. In 1619 the ardently Catholic Ferdinand II, king of Bohemia and Hungary, was deposed in Bohemia but elected emperor. He was replaced in Bohemia by Friedrich V of the Palatinate, the head of the Protestant Union.

Although the Union was soon dissolved, the conflicts intensified and broadened in widening religious and political gyres, which gradually involved the French and the Swedes along with Spain, England, and other countries. In 1624, losing in the war against the Protestant forces and Count Ernst von Mansfeld's mercenary corps, Ferdinand II accepted the offer of Albrecht von Wallenstein (1583–1634), the duke of Friedland—a Bohemian nobleman and convert to Catholicism grown fabulously wealthy through two marriages and shrewd speculations—to support the empire with an army raised at his own expense. Wallenstein's campaigns were so successful, and his enhancement in the empire so precipitous, that the Catholic princes—notably Maximilian of Bavaria along with the Spanish contingent at the imperial court in Vienna—became fearful and forced his removal from his generalship at the Electoral Diet of Regensburg in 1630. (In Schiller's play the place-name "Regenspurg" is a frequently recurring code word for Wallenstein's resentment against the emperor.) Wallenstein retired to his estates, where he maintained a notoriously magnificent lifestyle. Then King Gustavus Adolphus of Sweden, who had allied himself with the German Protestants and was hailed as their liberator, overwhelmed the Catholic forces, killing General Tilly of the Catholic League in the process, and moved as a conqueror rapidly to the south. Urgently recalled by the emperor, Wallenstein quickly raised a new army and met Gustavus Adolphus in the fall of 1632 at the Battle of Lützen, where the king was killed even though the Catholic armies lost the battle. After a further year of successful campaigning, Wallenstein withdrew his army to Bohemia for the winter of 1633–34, where it was rumored that he was negotiating secretly with Sweden and the Protestant state of Saxony to establish, over the emperor's objections, a peace with religious freedom in a unified Germany. Betrayed to Vienna by one of his officers, Octavio Piccolomini, Wallenstein was assassinated at Eger on 25 February 1634, with the full consent of the emperor.

Schiller was intimately acquainted with the history of the Thirty

Years' War and had studied the principal sources for the popular five-part *History of the Thirty Years' War* (1791–93) which he wrote while a professor of history at the University of Jena. Perhaps his greatest difficulty lay in the reduction and organization of the mass of material at his disposal. Initially he had planned to write a heroic epic (*Heldengedicht*) on the topic, focusing on Gustavus Adolphus.[16] But with a shrewd awareness of his own strengths and weaknesses, he quickly decided to cast the material in dramatic form and in the process shifted his focus from the Swedish king to Wallenstein, whose character he regarded with a cool detachment. The trilogy as finally published is centripetal in its structure, moving from the periphery on the outskirts of Pilsen, in Bohemia, where his followers are encamped, to its conclusion in the nearby town of Eger, where Wallenstein is murdered two days later.[17] But the organization is also symbolically illuminating because it exposes us, long before we actually meet Wallenstein, to the factors that bind his followers to him—and, as we gradually realize, shows that the seemingly all-powerful leader is utterly dependent on those around him.

The poetic "Prolog," which Schiller composed especially for the premiere of *Wallenstein's Camp* in Weimar in October 1798, reminds the audience of the background to the action involving this national hero. After sixteen years of devastating war, the empire is a vast battleground, its cities desolate and its trade a shambles.

> Auf diesem finstern Zeitgrund malet sich
> Ein Unternehmen kühnen Übermuts
> Und ein verwegener Charakter ab.
> (91–93)

(Against this gloomy temporal background an enterprise of daring arrogance outlines itself, and a bold character.)

An idol to his troops and a scourge as conquering general, he is the main support of an emperor who fears him because, despite his spectacular rise, his untamed ambition remains insatiate. While factionalism has made his image controversial, the poet promises to bring him closer as a human being to the audience's eyes and hearts.[18]

Wallenstein's Camp is a bold stroke of literary genius, in its form a remarkable anticipation of twentieth-century epic theater. If he hoped to win the audience's sympathy for a man regarded by many as a traitor, Schiller knew, it was essential to justify the love and admiration that his troops and the populace felt for him. Wallenstein—while like Achilles in the *Iliad* omnipresent as a force in the minds of everyone—does not appear here in person, nor are any individuals mentioned by name. The cast of characters lists only categories: snipers, dragoons and cuirassiers, foot soldiers, Croatians, citizens, a peasant, a recruit, a Capuchin monk, a sutler, and various other camp followers. "Here are all the wild lawless spirits of Europe assembled within the circuit of a single trench," writes Carlyle. "Violent, tempestuous, unstable is the life they lead."[19] In 1100 lines of the doggerel known as *Knittelvers*—hence as long as *The Libation Bearers*—and in a rapid succession of scenes not divided into acts, Schiller permits this motley band to present themselves in all their violence and generosity, to give voice to their lives and dreams, to express the desire for freedom that attracts them to the ranks of mercenary soldiers.

From all their camp talk, with its eating and gambling and singing and gossiping and crude jesting, emerges gradually the soldiers' myth of their charismatic leader, Wallenstein, along with rumors about his plots as well as the intrigues mounted against him. We learn that he has risen too high for the comfort of his enemies in Vienna. Accordingly orders have come from the emperor for Wallenstein to dispatch eight of his regiments to the Netherlands—ostensibly on a mission to accompany the Spanish Infante but in reality to weaken his army in Bohemia. His troops want to support Wallenstein. Not only does their good pay come from him and not from the emperor but his military triumphs have given them every reason for pride. Indeed, were it not for their love of Wallenstein, they would never have given their service to Ferdinand's cause. At the same time, their loyalties are tested because, after all, they have sworn allegiance to the emperor. We hear further of Wallenstein's blind faith in astrology, of the abnormal sensitivity to sound that contributes ultimately to his downfall, and of the incredible luck with which Fortune seems to favor him—no small virtue in the eyes of such a superstitious lot as his soldiers. His authority is absolute: he can make war or conclude peace, confiscate money and property, condemn and pardon. The only discordant note is sounded by the Capuchin monk, who—before he is driven off by the angry soldiers—preaches against their beloved general, suggesting that, like the biblical Peter, Wallenstein is about to deny his lord and master.

So powerful are these "immortal scenes"[20] that Mme de Staël, who attended a performance of *Wallenstein's Camp*, reported that she had the sensation of actually being in the midst of an army— an army of partisans, where everything was livelier and less disciplined than in an army of regular troops.[21] Above all, this first part of the trilogy offers us an unmediated impression of the basis for Wallenstein's success: he has the unqualified respect and support of his soldiers, whose loyalty is to their general and not to any cause. Indeed, this army of mercenaries recruited from every corner of Europe is so utterly disparate that it is held together only by the force of Wallenstein's personality. It emerges later that this affection is reciprocal: Wallenstein remembers the name and circumstances of every soldier whom he has met face to face. As Schiller remarks in the "Prolog," it is his very power that seduces his heart: only his camp explains his crime.

> Denn seine Macht ists, die sein Herz verführt,
> Sein Lager nur erkläret sein Verbrechen.
>
> (117–18)

WALLENSTEIN'S DELAY

With *The Piccolominis,* which begins according to Schiller's principle of simultaneity while the *Camp* scenes are taking place outside, the action moves into the town of Pilsen, where Wallenstein's officers are quartered. The action—a conventional five-act play in blank verse—focuses for the most part on the political loyalties of the officers themselves, many of them "new men," who have risen far beyond their station in Wallenstein's democratic ranks based on merit and loyalty; on the support of his wife, daughter, and sister, who have been summoned from their properties in Austria to join him;

and most important, as the title suggests, on the conflicting loyalties of the two Piccolominis: the political opposition of Octavio and the intense commitment of his son Max.

Wallenstein also makes his first appearance, albeit only in act 2, in a series of scenes that expose all the important issues and personal relationships of the play. Even before he enters, we are reminded of his fateful belief in the stars, for his astrologer Seni, who is overseeing the arrangement of the room, ensures that the numerologically favorable number of twelve chairs is present rather than an unlucky eleven. (It has been often remarked that astrology represents for Schiller a modern equivalent of ancient oracles of the sort, for instance, that sent Orestes to Argos.) Wallenstein enters with his wife, who with their daughter Thekla has just returned to Bohemia following years of absence while her husband was waging his wars across Germany. He first inquires about her observations at the court in Vienna and shares with her his plans for a politically advantageous marriage for their daughter. After telling him that her reception was cool, if formally correct, she reluctantly reports that powerful factions are urging the emperor to dismiss him for a second time. Here we get the first indication of Wallenstein's own feelings: he cries vehemently that they are compelling him, forceably and against his will, to act. Despite this first indication of his delaying tactics and reluctance to make a decision, we still have no clear sense of the reasons underlying them.

His daughter, whom he has not seen since she was eight years old, is brought in and soon thereafter his young friend, Max Piccolomini, who has escorted mother and daughter back to Bohemia. In his sole reliance on the stars and his blindness to human interests outside his own, Wallenstein does not realize that the two idealistic young people have fallen deeply in love—an affair that would not at all conform to his goal of an important matrimonial match for his daughter.

His brother-in-law and close supporter Terzky comes in (2.5) and reports that several of the officers Wallenstein has summoned to a meeting at Pilsen have declined to come, and warns him that other will break away "if you continue to delay." (The vocable *zögern*, "to delay," occurs frequently here and in later scenes.) Moreover, Wallenstein's go-between with the Swedish army reports that the Swedes are beginning to fear that his negotiations with them are simply a diversion to conceal an intention to ally himself with Saxony against Sweden. When Terzky, the opportunistic *Realpolitiker,* urges his brother-in-law to give the Swedes the territory they demand, Wallenstein becomes indignant and provides the first disclosure of his own plans. He has no intention, he insists, of betraying Germany to foreign powers in order to obtain benefits for himself. As for the Saxons, who are also becoming impatient with his delays, Wallenstein suggests that he is deceiving all of them. Who among them knows him well enough to penetrate his innermost thoughts? He still recalls bitterly his mistreatment by the emperor at Regensburg. "*If* I so desired, I could pay him back in kind." But— and this is the decisive factor—what Wallenstein enjoys is the knowledge that he has the power to move in any one of several directions. Whether or not or how he will actually make use of this power, neither Terzky nor anyone else can know.

> Der Kaiser, es ist wahr,
> Hat übel mich behandelt!—*Wenn* ich wollte,
> Ich könnt ihm recht viel Böses dafür tun.
> Es macht mir Freude, meine Macht zu kennen;
> Ob ich sie wirklich brauchen werde, *davon,* denk ich,
> Weißt *du* nicht mehr zu sagen als ein andrer.
> (865–70)

("The emperor, it is true, has treated me badly. *If* I wanted, I could do him much evil in return. It gives me pleasure to know my power. Whether I shall really use it—about *that,* I believe, *you* know no more than anyone else.")

In sum, all his delaying tactics—the winter quarters in Bohemia well away from the battlefronts in Bavaria, the gathering of his considerable forces, the removal of his family from the possibility of being seized as hostages, the tentative negotiations with the enemy—all serve one purpose: to give him flexibility and the sense that he has the option and the power to move in any direction he pleases. Theoretically, he believes, he can remain loyal to the emperor; he can link himself with the invading forces; or he can maintain his independence from both and establish a religiously liberated Germany free from the pressures of Catholics and Protestants alike. This unwillingness to submit his individualism to any authority is the true mark of his heroic temperament. When Terzky and his confidant Illo demand that he stop temporizing and either obey the emperor's command or make a clean break with the imperial court, he tells them that the time is not yet ripe; the stars have not yet reached their proper conjunction. But he asks them as a precaution to gather the signatures of his assembled officers on a statement of loyalty and support for him, regardless of the direction in which he chooses to move.

At this point the emperor's envoy, Questenberg, enters to lay out the imperial accusations and demands. Instead of following up and exploiting his victories, Wallenstein has wintered in Bohemia with his troops while the enemy has moved south into Franconia and Bavaria, frightening all good Catholics. Wallenstein retorts that he was fully occupied with driving the enemy out of Silesia and that his troops deserved a much-needed respite. Questenberg demands that Wallenstein release the eight regiments to accompany the Spanish Infante to the Netherlands and that with his remaining army he hasten to liberate Regensburg from the Swedes. When Wallenstein threatens simply to give up his contract with the emperor and to release his army from their obligations, his officers are scandalized and plead with him to stay. As the act ends, Wallenstein tells his officers that Illo and Terzky know his will. He then disappears from the scene for the remainder of *The Piccolomini,* still under the illusion that he has freedom of action.

In fact, however, it is too late, for, as we soon learn, Wallenstein's freedom of decision has already been undermined. Questenberg has brought with him a royal decree removing Wallenstein from his command and replacing him, at least temporarily, with Octavio Piccolomini. Since this fact is not revealed as a certainty until act 5, much of the action takes on an aspect of tragic irony. As *The Piccolomini* opens, Wallenstein's chief co-conspirators—the generals Illo and Isolani along with Buttler, a captain of the dragoons—are discussing the meeting to which Wallenstein has summoned all his principal officers. The absence of two raises the first suspicion that a counterplot is underway. But their conversation also reveals how Wallenstein has gained the loyalty of his supporters: he has satisfied Isolani's creditors, and he has promised Buttler advancement to a generalship. When Octavio and Questenberg appear, the conversation exposes further differences between Wallenstein and the imperial court. Questenberg is dismayed to discover the degree of loyalty to Wallenstein, which has been underestimated in Vienna.

The appearance of Octavio's son, Max, introduces a new element into the emotional equation, for Max is still young enough, as Joseph Conrad puts it in *Lord Jim* (chap. 17), "to behold at every turn the magnificence that besets our insignificant footsteps in good and evil." This first of two major dialogues between father and son depicts a classic opposition of naive youthful idealism and mature experienced *Realpolitik*. When Max argues that Wallenstein is capable of getting the best out of every individual, his father points out that the commander's success is nothing but a shrewd assessment and exploitation of human desires. (And Wallenstein's subsequent dealings with Max, Buttler, and others does expose his cynical abuse of their confidence and trust.) Max exclaims that the living oracle in Wallenstein's heart is more trustworthy than dead books and old orders. Octavio replies that the established order should not be dismissed lightly: it provides the stability that restrains the arbitrary acts of the hasty individual. Max, who on his recent journey has for the first time in his young life seen a peaceful land untouched by war, believes that Wallenstein should be permitted to make an immediate peace, to which his father and Questenberg object realistically that in politics and diplomacy lofty goals cannot be rapidly achieved. By the time the first act ends, we have been exposed to the principal opposing forces—the calculating opportunism of the generals and the youthful idealism of Max versus the emperor's demands for obedience, loyalty, and continuity.

The third act belongs mainly to Max and Thekla, "these two angelic beings" according to Thomas Carlyle,[22] and "créatures célestes" in the words of Mme de Staël, "who traverse all the storms of political passions while preserving in their souls love and truth."[23] While Max, as we have seen, is bound by blind adoration to Wallenstein, whose lofty dreams of peace he admires with all his youthful fervor, Thekla, fresh from the cloister, sees not only the military followers but even her father with eyes uncluttered by experience of the world. "Don't trust anybody here but me," she tells him (3.5). "I saw it right away; they have a purpose." Her instincts are proved correct when the Countess Terzky discourages her love for Max, pointing out that her father has different plans in mind for her, the richest heiress in Europe.

Act 4 features the feast at which the assembled officers are supposed to sign the letter of support for Wallenstein. Wallenstein, it recapitulates, had intended to resign from the emperor's service because of repeated offenses to his honor, but was moved by their pleas to remain and not to leave without their consent. In return they promise, collectively and individually, to remain loyal and true to him and to sacrifice their last drop of blood for him *insofar as their oath of allegiance to the emperor will allow.* Before dinner the declaration is circulated in this form for the scrutiny of the officers; but later, when they are too drunk to notice, the schemers—Terzky, Illo, and Isolani—give them a different copy to sign, in which the final clause has been removed.

Max, distracted by his earlier conversation with Thekla, refuses to sign. Shortly thereafter (act 5) his father exposes the plot, warning his son that he is being deceived. Wallenstein is planning to steal the army from the emperor and hand it over to the enemy. Max still refuses to believe any ill of his admired friend, arguing that Wallenstein is simply trying to force the emperor to accept peace terms that are offensive to Vienna. In this extended dialogue, which brings out again all the contrasts between father and son, between maturity and youth, experience and idealism, tradition and experiment, Octavio recounts every detail of the plot—the reasons for the assembly at Pilsen, the significance of the absent generals, the substitution of the edited declaration—but Max refuses to accept the facts and finds his father's own behavior contemptible. "It's not always possible in real life," Octavio informs him, "to keep oneself as childlike-pure as our innermost voice teaches us." In this case, he continues, duty requires them to serve the emperor, regardless of the heart's urgings. In a final gesture of trust he shows Max an open letter bearing the imperial seal, in which Wallenstein is condemned and outlawed—an extreme action, he explains, that will not be taken if Wallenstein will agree to lay down his command peaceably and retreat into an honorable exile in one of his palaces. He promises not to make use of the document until Max himself agrees that Wallenstein has committed a deed that irrefutably attests high treason. But Max, in the blindness of his youthful enthusiasm, exclaims "Your judgment can err, but not my heart."

At this moment a messenger arrives to announce that Wallenstein's intermediary to the Swedes has been caught bearing incriminating letters. Octavio asks Max if this is not proof enough of Wallenstein's guilt, but Max storms out of the room, cursing Octavio's "statecraft" ("Staatskunst") and intending to confront Wallenstein face to face. "Before the day is over it must become clear whether I am to lose my friend or my father."

WALLENSTEIN'S HESITATION

Again it is useful to make a distinction between hesitation and delay. Wallenstein's delaying tactics, which have been going on for over a year, resulted from a conscious choice. A veritable control freak, unwilling to leave anything to chance, he has been waiting for the auspicious moment and trying to keep all his options open: loyalty to the emperor, treasonous alliance with the Swedes, manipulation of the Swedes to force a peaceful settlement on the empire, or inglorious withdrawal to a private life. His absence from the *Camp* and his brief appearance in *The Piccolomini* amount to a symbolic reminder of these delays. Now, as we learn from the opening words of *Wallenstein's Death*, which overlaps in time with the closing scenes of *The Piccolomini*, the moment has arrived: the planets, and notably his two good-luck stars ("Segenssterne"), Jupiter and Venus, are in the proper conjunction. It is no longer the time for brooding and meditating, he tells his astrologer; "it's time for action" ("Nicht Zeit ist mehr zu brüten und zu sinnen, . . .—Jetzt muß / Gehandelt werden").

But Wallenstein's jubilation is abruptly shattered when Terzky rushes in to report (as we know already from Octavio in *Piccolomini*) that his intermediary to the Swedes has been captured. "You must go forward," Illo tells him, "for you can no longer go back" (1.3). Illo and Terzky are actually delighted with the turn of events because they have grown weary of Wallenstein's interminable temporizations. But Wallenstein is dismayed to realize that his gamelike freedom of choice has vanished.[24] "What? Am I now supposed to fulfill it in earnest because I trifled too freely with the thought?"

> Wie? Sollt ichs nun in Ernst erfüllen müssen,
> Weil ich zu frei gescherzt mit dem Gedanken?
> (112–13)

Indignantly he asserts that he is not accustomed to be led blindly by chance. His great monologue (I.4) expresses his frustration and the hesitation that now governs his inaction.

> Wärs möglich? Könnt ich nicht mehr, wie ich wollte?
> Nicht mehr zurück, wie mirs beliebt? Ich müßte
> Die Tat *vollbringen,* weil ich sie *gedacht.*

("Could it be possible? That I can no longer act as I wish? That I can no longer go back as I choose? That I have to *complete* the deed simply because I *thought* it?")

> Es war nicht
> Mein Ernst, beschloßne Sache war es nie.
> In dem Gedanken bloß gefiel ich mir;
> Die Freiheit reizte mich und das Vermögen.

("It wasn't my serious intention, it was never a decided thing. I merely enjoyed the thought of it; the freedom to do it tempted me and the capability.")

Standing in profound meditation ("er bleibt tiefsinnig stehen"), he realizes that his enemies will assume that his playful dreams amounted to a coherent plan. He himself has woven the web from which only an act of violence can now free him. Yet he still believes in his own innocence.

The Swedish emissary Wrangel (not to be confused with the captured intermediary) arrives with the last-minute hope of a solution. The Swedes, namely, promise him what he has wanted: the crown of Bohemia. But they have certain concerns. Can Wallenstein actually persuade his armies to join in such a drastic step as treason against the Holy Roman Empire? Wallenstein maintains his absolute, if somewhat contemptuous, faith in his troops: the riffraff of Europe, they know no other lord but him. As proof, Wallenstein shows Wrangel the oath of allegiance signed by his generals the night before. Wrangel then states his terms: in return for the support of its army Sweden demands Wallenstein's immediate break with the emperor; and as a token of good faith he must seize Prague, disarm the Spanish regiments there, and hand it over to his new allies until Sweden has been recompensed for its support. At this demand Wallenstein balks. Despite Wrangel's argument that the negotiations have been going on for more than a year—the delay—and that immediate action is required for success, Wallenstein now hesitates.

After Wrangel's departure, he tells Terzky and Illo that nothing has been decided and that, on reflection, he would rather not do it. His confidants, astonished at this new turn of events, appeal to his sister, Countess Terzky—who has accurately been termed one of Schiller's "superwomen"[25]—, to persuade him to act. Wallenstein weasels, asking her to show him a way out of the pressures. But with a rhetorical skill that reminds us of Clytemnestra's eloquence and Electra's vehemence, she reminds him of the indignities he suffered at Regensburg and of his decisiveness in his past military campaigns as he stormed victoriously through Germany. Indeed, Wrangel had earlier compared him in ferocity to Attila and Pyrrhus (1.5: the same Pyrrhus as in *Hamlet*). She points out that all the astrological signs point to victory and that the very planets cry: "It's time!" Overwhelmed by her passion and her words, Wallenstein succumbs and sends a messenger to catch Wrangel. (Like Hamlet, he does not so much decide as allow himself to be pushed by circumstances into an action.)

The second act features Max Piccolomini in its opening and closing scenes. After Wallenstein has ordered Octavio to seize the two

disloyal generals and to take over the command of the Spanish regiments in Prague, Max rushes in and confronts him with the news
he has heard. He assures Wallenstein that he is prepared to follow
him into a departure from imperial service, but Wallenstein now reveals that he has been forced by circumstances to choose between
two evils. Since the court has determined his downfall, he has decided to anticipate by taking the offensive against the emperor.
Max, stunned at this confession, says that Wallenstein is forcing him
to make a choice between his revered friend and his own heart. The
idea of a renewed war is intolerable in the light of Wallenstein's pro-
gram of peace. He would still follow Wallenstein anywhere—except
into treason. Wallenstein tells the young idealist some home truths.
While the mind is wide, the world is narrow (*"Eng* ist die Welt, und
das Gehirn ist *weit"*). In words that echo Octavio's, he reminds Max
that the real world belongs to the evil spirit, not the good one, and
it is impossible to maintain a pure soul in the service of reality.
When Max urges him to return to his loyal commitment, Wallenstein—who has delayed and hesitated so long—tells him, twice for
emphasis, that it's too late. "We act because we must."

Now the web begins to tighten around Wallenstein in a brilliant
succession of brief scenes. Terzky reports that Wrangel left before
the messengers could catch him and tries again to warn Wallenstein
against Octavio. Octavio, meanwhile, is busy undermining the other
supporters. When Isolani reports that many officers do not feel
bound by the oath they were tricked into signing, Octavio shows
him his own patent of command from the emperor, and Isolani
quickly capitulates. Buttler gives in with equal alacrity when Octavio
proves to him that Wallenstein was in reality scornful about him and
had no intention of supporting his bid for a title of nobility. In their
final confrontation Max tells Octavio that he feels betrayed by both
his friend and his father. Incapable of betraying either Wallenstein
or the emperor, he swears that he will never dishonor his father or
his own heart.

The third act presents a sequence of disenchantments. Thekla
and her mother are dismayed to learn of Wallenstein's treasonous
plans. Wallenstein, still deceived about the loyalties of those surrounding him, is indignant to hear that Max aspires to the hand of

his daughter. Then Terzky and Illo report that the other generals have all departed. When Wallenstein is finally convinced of Octavio's betrayal, he sinks heavily into a chair in despair, unable to comprehend how these things could have taken place against the predictions of the stars. "Where nature sways out of her boundaries, all science goes astray" ("Wo die Natur aus ihren Grenzen wanket, / Da irret alle Wissenschaft," 1673–74). By this reasoning he is able to persuade himself that he, the betrayer, has been betrayed by all the others. Further blows strike him: Prague is lost, other regiments have deserted, and along with his accomplices he has been outlawed. Paradoxically, these shocks strengthen Wallenstein, who exclaims that he's the same man he always was. "When head and limbs are separated, then will be revealed where the soul dwelled." ("Wenn Haupt und Glieder sich trennen, / Da wird sich zeigen, wo die Seele wohnte," 1817–18). Ten cuirassiers from the Pappenheim regiment enter to demand an explanation. Wallenstein tries to persuade them that he was only pretending to negotiate with the Swedes in order to force the emperor to declare a peace. But when Buttler announces that Terzky's troops have torn down the imperial eagle and replaced it with Wallenstein's insignia, the Pappenheims march out without a word. Max comes in search of Thekla, and Wallenstein appeals to him out of love to stay by his side. Max, aware that his blind trust in his own heart is of little use in the mire of reality, is at a loss, but Thekla, undistracted from her idealism by such waverings, urges him to follow his initial instincts. Thereupon Max, whose most frequent word in all his speeches has been "rein" ("pure"), rushes out—"Whoever goes with me should be prepared to die!"

The scene shifts to Eger (act 4), where Wallenstein seeks safety and hopes to regroup his forces. As Buttler plots to murder Wallenstein that evening, news arrives that Max and his Pappenheims have been killed in a gallant but hopeless attack on the advancing Swedish forces. Learning of her lover's valiant death, Thekla resolves to end her own life on his grave and steals out of town. Buttler wants to act quickly before the citizens, who are sympathetic to the Protestant cause, can come to Wallenstein's assistance. His henchmen, Deveroux and Macdonald, worry about the soldiers' superstition that Wallenstein is "frozen"—that is, invulnerable. But

Buttler assures them that, because of his dislike of noise, he sleeps
alone and far from any bodyguard. Meanwhile Wallenstein, sad-
dened at the news of Max's death, reminisces with his old friend
Gordon about their own youth. The astrologer enters to warn Wallenstein to leave Eger: the signs are terrible and signify destruction.
But Wallenstein is unperturbed. With painfully honest insight into
his own character, he weighs for one final time his vacillation between ambition and ethics, treason and loyalty.[26]

> Hätt ich vorhergewußt, was nun geschehn,
> Daß es den liebsten Freund mir würde kosten,
> Und hätte mir das Herz wie jetzt gesprochen—
> Kann sein, ich hätte mich bedacht—kann sein
> Auch nicht.
>
> (3657–61)

(If I had known before what now has happened and that it would cost
me my dearest friend, and if my heart had spoken to me then as it does
now, then perhaps I would have thought differently—and perhaps not.)

Then he leaves the room, and the drama, with the ironically unwit-
ting remark, "I think that I'll have a long sleep,"

After Wallenstein's departure Buttler reports that Illo and Terzky
have been killed. The murderers follow Wallenstein into his room.
(Gordon's words remind us of Hamlet's reflections as he watches
Claudius at prayer: "Oh, his heart is still turned toward mundane
things; he's not prepared to step before his God.") When the Countess Terzky learns that her husband and Wallenstein are both dead
and that Wallenstein's wife is dying, she swallows poison, finding "a
free courageous death more decent than a dishonored life." Octavio enters and learns that Wallenstein has been murdered; he exclaims in a tradition extending from Pontius Pilate to the aged
Faust, "I am not guilty of this horrible deed." As the play ends, Gordon with a reproachful look hands him an imperial communiqué
naming him *Prince* Piccolomini.

A great deal has been written about Wallenstein's hesitation at least
since Mme de Staël, who observed that the most universally repeated criticism of Schiller's play in France stemmed from Wallen-

stein's character, which is "superstitieux, incertain, irrésolu" and hence not compatible with "le modèle héroïque" expected in a role of that sort.[27] Schiller's friend Humboldt reported, in the epistolary essay cited in the first paragraph above, that he had heard Wallenstein's indecisive temporization criticized although it struck him as entirely appropriate. And Hegel, in an early reaction (around 1800) to the first performances in Weimar, saw the entire drama—correctly in my opinion—as the play of "indeterminacy in the midst of sheer determinacies" ("Unbestimmtsein mitten unter lauter Bestimmtheiten").[28] Seeking to maintain his independence among friends and enemies with their own agendas, Wallenstein must finally see his indeterminacy give way tragically to determinacy. As we noted above, his hesitation has recently been interpreted to have various meanings, ranging from a shrewd act of military tactics to a statement of aesthetic detachment. In addition, critics have emphasized the role of Wallenstein's melancholy temperament.[29] The motivation is surely as complex as we are entitled to expect from a dramatist as profound as Schiller. Indeed, it might be suggested that no one has analyzed the conditions of Wallenstein's temporizations more acutely than Kierkegaard in *Either/Or,* where he distinguishes aesthetic choice from ethical choice.

> When a man deliberates aesthetically upon a multitude of life's problems . . . he does not easily get one either/or, but a whole multiplicity, because the self-determining factor in the choice is not ethically accentuated, and because when one does not choose absolutely one chooses only for the moment, and therefore can choose something different the next moment.[30]

The only interpretation that I find unconvincing claims that his hesitation is relatively unimportant for the action.[31]

For we can now see that Wallenstein's pattern of delay and hesitation bears a remarkable resemblance to that in *Hamlet.* Had Hamlet slain Claudius immediately when he had the chance, he would in all likelihood have prevented a succession of deaths, including his own. Similarly, if Wallenstein had acted immediately at the beginning of *Wallenstein's Death,* he could have prevented the deaths of Max, Thekla, his wife, his sister, Terzky and Illo, and himself. True, he would not have become king like Hamlet, but he had been assured an honorable exile on his vast properties if only he would lay down his command and withdraw in peace. Even if he had committed himself to the Swedes, most of the deaths—though perhaps not those of Max and Thekla—might have been avoided. The confusion stems, I believe, from the common failure to distinguish between *delay* and *hesitation*. To be sure, the reasons for Wallenstein's delay and hesitation are quite different from those of Hamlet,[32] and in the last analysis we are unable to make any final judgment on his character and motivation. But the similarity in the structure of their behavior alerts us to the factors that generate their delay and hesitation.

WAR AS PARADIGM

In his poetic "Prolog" Schiller reminds his audience that they are standing "at the century's sober end, where reality itself becomes poetry, where we see before our eyes the battle of powerful natures and a great goal, and where a struggle is going on for humanity's great objects, for power and for freedom."

> Und jetzt an des Jahrhunderts ernstem Ende,
> Wo selbst die Wirklichkeit zur Dichtung wird,
> Wo wir den Kampf gewaltiger Naturen
> Und ein bedeutend Ziel vor Augen sehn,
> Und um der Menschheit große Gegenstände,
> Um Herrschaft und um Freiheit wird gerungen.
> (61–66)

In these times, he continues, one sees "the firm old form" ("die alte feste Form") fall apart, which 150 years earlier had been presented to Europe's kingdoms by the Peace of Westphalia, ending thirty miserable years of war.

The analogy suggested here—between two eras racked by war, where powerful personalities battle for power and freedom in the name of lofty goals—was stated quite clearly in Schiller's *History of*

the Thirty Years' War. Written in the immediate aftermath of the
French Revolution, Schiller's *History* also reflected his fear that the
era introduced by the events in France might again prelude a
lengthy period of European war. As in late eighteenth-century
France, the Thirty Years' War was set off when the haughtiness of
the Bohemian princes caused them to refuse to acknowledge the
spirit of freedom ("Geist der Freiheit")[33] and legitimate demands
of the people—in that case, the demands for freedom of religion
as vouchsafed by an imperial letter. The "Bohemian rebels" therefore took action in a scene as dramatic, if not as bloody, as the storm-
ing of the Bastille: in the infamous "defenestration" they tossed two
of the offending princes out the window of the royal palace in
Prague. These incidents, vividly recounted in book 1 of Schiller's
History and also taking place in a neighboring country on Germany's periphery, initiate the escalations that gradually bring
armies from many countries into central Germany, making it the
principal war zone—a development eerily foreshadowing the revolutionary wars that again were to last almost thirty years and to
be waged extensively in German states. Again the war pitted the
ideologies of revolutionary freedom and the conservatism of an
ancien régime against each other. And, though Schiller in 1799
could only dimly sense it and did not live to see it, the new war
again brought mighty military personalities into conflict: not Gustavus Adolphus and Wallenstein, the heroes of his *History,* but
Napoleon and the great leaders of the nations that rose up to oppose him.

It has been frequently remarked that *Wallenstein* reflects the most
urgent themes of the 1790s.[34] In the northern German states,
which from the Treaty of Basel in 1795 until the humiliating Pruss-
ian defeat at Jena-Auerstedt in 1806 enjoyed a relatively peaceful
decade, thoughtful persons were able to contemplate with an almost Wallenstein-like aesthetic detachment the implications of the
startling new political developments surging out from France. Im-
manuel Kant, Johann Fichte, and Wilhelm von Humboldt among
others devoted important books and essays to the consideration of
the legitimate role of government (Humboldt's "Ideas toward an
Attempt to Determine the Boundaries of the Effectiveness of the

State," 1792), the possibility of peace (Kant's *At the Sign of Eternal Peace,* 1795), the nature of law (Fichte's *Basis of Natural Law,* 1796), and other burning issues: the relationship between power and freedom, the role and responsibilities of morality in politics, the rights of the individual in the face of public demands. And Schiller, especially in the first ten of his letters, *On the Aesthetic Education of Man* (1795), written under the immediate impact of developments in France, analyzed the collapse of social values and the fragmentation of the individual in an age that has been subjected to the tyrannical yoke of necessity.

The Revolution and the subsequent Terror of the early 1790s exposed the enormous chasm between philosophical ideals and political reality. By attacking the power structure, therefore, Wallenstein simultaneously attacks forms of thought. It is typical of Schiller, as a philosopher of history, that he exposes and intellectualizes the historical processes.[35] Wallenstein's dream of a unified Germany anticipated the longing for unification shared by many German thinkers during the Napoleonic Era (e.g., Novalis in his impassioned speech *Christendom or Europe,* 1799). Wallenstein's failure to understand that his power depended on the support of his followers prefigured the fate of Danton, Robespierre, and other demagogues of the Revolution who were ultimately overthrown by the very partisans whose emotions they had stirred up. Indeed, *Wallenstein's Camp* with its scenes of the common people is unimaginable without the experience of the French Revolution; certainly nothing similar had ever before been seen on European stages. When Octavio Piccolomini (in the second play) warns his son Max that "civil war is flaring up, the most unnatural of all" (5.1), Schiller's audience surely thought of recent events in France. And Wallenstein's words (in *Wallenstein's Death*) must also have sent tremors through the first audience in Weimar in 1799: "The fulfillment of the ages has come, mayor. The lofty will fall and the lowly are rising . . . a new order of affairs is being initiated" (4.3). Stephen Spender suggested that Schiller had to reach into the past of the Thirty Years' War to find a hero large enough to represent those historical forces which, in the present, tend to diminish and "denature" the great man.[36] As Buttler puts it in his words to the military commander of Eger:

> Es denkt der Mensch die freie Tat zu tun,
> Umsonst! Er ist das Spielwerk nur der blinden
> Gewalt, die aus der eignen Wahl ihm schnell
> Die furchtbare Notwendigkeit erschafft.
>
> (*Wallenstein's Death,* 5.8)

("A man believes that he is carrying out a free act. In vain! He is merely the plaything of blind violence, which from his own free choice quickly creates frightful necessity.")

Despite the death and transfiguration of its hero,[37] the drama ends in profound ambiguity. The youthful idealists, Max and Thekla, have been ground to bits and destroyed by the warring forces of political reality, and in the last analysis no moral authority is left intact. Wallenstein's motivation is murky, and the agents of empire are, if not corrupt, at least ignoble. This is the political reality of the world as Schiller saw it—in 1634 as well as 1799. Wallenstein's delays and hesitation express his own tragic bewilderment in the face of a new reality where the traditional authorities and loyalties have lost their meaning and the individual is cast into an almost existential anxiety.

6

Wavering Heroes, from Scotland to Spain

"I want a hero," Byron announces when opening the first canto of *Don Juan* (1819), written exactly twenty years after Schiller's *Wallenstein,*

> an uncommon want,
> When every year and month sends forth a new one,
> Till, after cloying the gazettes with cant,
> The age discovers he is not the true one.

We miss the point if we take it simply as a joke when Byron decides to turn to "our ancient friend Don Juan." For the absence of a hero in the sense conventional since Homer speaks precisely to the dilemma of an age moving from the feudal to the democratic, from the traditional to the industrial, from commonly shared values to independently asserted ones.

To make his point Byron catalogs two dozen recent English and French military heroes of the revolutionary wars, most of whose names are already forgotten. This public amnesia, he continues (1.5) exists mainly because their deeds were not recorded for posterity in poetry—as were, by implication, those of Aeneas, Orestes, Parzival, Hamlet, and Wallenstein.

> Brave men were living before Agamemnon
> And since, exceeding valorous and sage,
> A good deal like him too, though quite the same none;
> But then they shone not on the poet's page,
> And so have been forgotten.

Half a century later, Byron's lament was echoed by the historian Edgar Quinet in the first line of his novel *Merlin l'enchanteur* (1860): "Et moi aussi je cherche un homme, un héros!" Why, he wonders in his preface, have contemporary French writers been unable to produce literary works to match the "vast inventions" of the Middle Ages? Because the public is said to be too feeble, too corrupt, too trite, lacking the stamina to traverse vast horizons.[1] Accordingly he too turns to "the tradition of Merlin, which reaches back to our earliest origins and has grown across the centuries down to our own days, reflecting the coloration of each age." The question is directly relevant to our concern. Before a hero can hesitate, he must be a "hero"—and not simply in the derivative sense designating the principal male figure in a literary work, but in Hegel's sense of an exemplary *heros,* the vocable by which he defined "individuals who out of the independence of their character and their free will take upon themselves and complete the entirety of an action and in whom it therefore appears as personal conviction if they carry out what is right and ethical."[2] Such heroes, Hegel continues, become the creators of states in which law and order are recognized as their individual achievement. (It is noteworthy that Hegel prefers the Greco-Latin term *heros* to the German equivalent *Held.*)

THE WAVERING HERO

Even before Byron, and long before Quinet, another writer had come to grips with the issue of the hero in modern times. Twice on the first page of *Waverley* (1814), and repeatedly throughout, Sir Walter Scott refers explicitly to "my hero" or "our hero."[3] But, as his name implies, Scott's "hero" wavers, vacillates, and hesitates—a natural tendency exacerbated by his unstructured education and the random reading of his youth. The author speaks of his "wavering

and unsettled habit of mind" (31). His Scottish friend Fergus complains that he is "blown about with every wind of doctrine" (237).
When he is torn between remaining in the Highlands and returning to England, "his mind wavered between these plans" (181). A
newspaper report on his dishonor—punning on the name of the
family estate: "the *Wavering Honour* of W-v-r-l-y H-n-r" (126)—suggests that his vacillation is endemic. And one of the novel's earliest
readers, Crabb Robinson, noted that Waverley, "as his name was
probably intended to indicate, is ever hesitating between two kings
and two mistresses."[4] Accordingly, one scholar describes him in a
chapter entitled "The Passive Hero":

> The hero of the Waverley Novels is seldom a leader. He is always a po-
> tential leader, because of his rank as a gentleman. He represents, how-
> ever, a social ideal, and acts or refrains from acting according to the
> accepted morality of his public.[5]

In sum, Scott's hero is typical not through his eminence, like our
earlier examples, but precisely because he is a decent, average man
of his time.[6] Like Thackeray's heroes as characterized by Mario
Praz, he is "not an exceptional man; he is, rather, a man just like
other men who only 'in the presence of the great occasion' is capable of showing his superiority over other men; when the critical
moment is over, he falls back into normality, into mediocrity."[7]

Scott's *Waverley*—according to Goethe to be reckoned among
"the best works ever written in the world,"[8] regarded by a modern
authority as "arguably Scott's greatest,"[9] and certainly, as the first
true historical novel, of inestimable influence on European and
American literature of the nineteenth century—is of particular interest here because of its parallels to *Wallenstein,* a work with which
Scott was intimately familiar, both in the German and in Coleridge's
translation (which he held to be better than Schiller's original).[10]
I am not suggesting that Scott's plot or characterization were in any
way influenced by Schiller's drama. But certain conspicuous parallels enable us to make useful comparisons and to ascertain how
these two works, written respectively at the beginning and at the end
of the Napoleonic Wars, reflect changes in popular understanding

of the heroic. (Scott himself, in *Paul's Letters,* compared Napoleon
to Wallenstein, notably in his belief in the stars.)

Waverley and *Wallenstein* are works about peoples in a conflict
over religion, politics, and culture—a conflict exacerbated in both
cases by the invasion of a leader from abroad. In *Waverley* the fictional action is set against the background of the ill-fated Rising of
1745–1746, when the Pretender Charles Stuart—Bonnie Prince
Charlie—came to Scotland from his exile in France and, aided by
disgruntled Highland clans, sought to overthrow the Hanoverian
rule that had been imposed on Scotland since the Treaty of Union
of 1707. Accordingly the novel pits North against South, Catholic/
High Church against Presbyterian/Puritan, Tory against Whig,
clan against kingdom, national independence against Union, community against society, primitive against civilized, feudal against
modern, tradition against progress, passion against reason, among
the various oppositions at work in the plot.[11] Thanks to Scott's genius, his novel succeeds in bringing these various factions and ideologies vividly to life through its huge cast of characters (not unlike
Schiller in *Wallenstein's Camp* and *The Piccolomini*). Binary oppositions are often represented by such pairs as Edward Waverley's Jacobite uncle Everard and his opportunistic Hanoverian father
Richard, the fiery Highland Jacobites Fergus Mac-Ivor and his sister Flora vis-à-vis the Hanoverian English Colonel Talbot and his
wife Lady Emily, or the blonde and brunette women of whom Scott
is so fond: the Lowland Rose and the Highland Flora.

Like Byron and Quinet, but also like the other authors discussed
in earlier chapters, Scott turned to the past for his heroes. As he explained in the frequently cited opening chapter of the novel,

> By fixing then the date of my story Sixty Years before this present 1st
> November, 1805, I would have my readers understand that they will
> meet in the following pages neither a romance of chivalry, nor a tale
> of modern manners; that my hero will neither have iron on his shoul-
> ders, as of yore, nor on the heels of his boots, as in the present fash-
> ion of Bond Street.

From this choice of an era, he continues, "the understanding critic
may farther presage, that the object of my tale is more a description

of men than manners" (4). While the novel is quite properly praised by historians precisely for its unparalleled description of the manners of 1745, in both England and Scotland,[12] Scott lavishes his considerable psychological insight on his figures' character.

The figure who most resembles the Hegelian hero (and the Wallenstein of his successful military campaigns) in his "ambition and love of rule," "patriarchal power," "military discipline" (92), and politically skillful manipulation of others, is not the titular hero but the fierce Highland chieftain Fergus Mac-Ivor, who like the Bohemian field marshal dies for his beliefs. "Fergus's brain was a perpetual work-shop of scheme and intrigue, of every possible kind and description. It was therefore often difficult to guess what line of conduct he might finally adopt upon any given occasion" (248). (His ancestor who, three centuries earlier, had been defeated in his quest for the chieftainship of his clan and moved south in search of new settlements, was called "a second Aeneas," 91; the *Aeneid* is one of the most frequently cited works in the text.) But unlike Wallenstein, Fergus—incited by a sister even more intense in her fervor than Countess Terzky—never wavers or hesitates in his beliefs or actions. On the very morning of his execution his thoughts are occupied with his Highland clan. "Would to God," he tells Waverley, "'I could bequeath to you my rights to the love and obedience of this primitive and brave race'" (325).

While Fergus resembles Wallenstein in military heroism, he is only one of the various aspects of the plot held together by Edward Waverley, who is able to do this precisely because his open-minded temperament and genuine human curiosity permit him to move freely among the radically differing groups he encounters on his journeys up and down England and Scotland. It has been calculated that, in the year and a half depicted in the novel, Edward travels over two thousand miles.[13] And this same temperament, as we shall see, puts him into a dilemma almost precisely like that faced by Wallenstein. The action of the novel begins and ends in the Scottish Lowlands—on the symbolic border, so to speak, between the various polarities at issue in the plot.

Edward is in no sense a commanding field marshal with a sovereign overview of men and events. His experiences at the Battle of

Prestonpans anticipate, rather, the confused wanderings of Stendhal's Fabrice del Dongo over the battlefield at Waterloo and Tolstoy's Pierre Bezukhov at Borodino. Raised at the southern English estate of Waverley-Honour by an affectionate uncle who had "inherited from his sires the whole train of tory or high-church predilections and prejudices" (6) and withdrawn from parliament "at the period of the Hanoverian accession" (21), Edward himself enjoys a temperament that is repeatedly called "romantic" and indulges, rather than in any systematic education, in reading Shakespeare, Cervantes, and Ariosto and in dreamy "castle-building" (chap. 5). (It has been suggested that his inability to act is a typical manifestation of the dreamlike state in which he drifts until his spiritual awakening late in the novel.)[14] Going to Edinburgh sometime late in 1744 or early in 1745 to gain military experience before inheriting the house of Waverley, he is favorably predisposed toward the romance of the ancient Scottish customs that he encounters there. In the summer of 1745 he takes a leave from military duty to visit his uncle's old friend Cosmo Bradwardine at Tully-Veolan on the Lowland border of the Perthshire Highlands, where he meets Bradwardine's fair daughter Rose, whose "very soul is in home, and in the discharge of all those quiet virtues of which home is the centre" (111). During his stay he eagerly seizes the opportunity to make a trip into the Highlands, where he encounters Fergus Mac-Ivor and his sister Flora, a dark-eyed enchantress who "was precisely the character to fascinate a youth of romantic imagination" (116). Reciting ballads recording the feats of ancient Gaelic heroes, Flora further excites Waverley to the allure of the heroic traditions. Waverley accompanies Fergus to a great stag hunt, unaware that it is the pretext for a meeting of the clan chieftains to plan their support of Prince Charles in the Jacobite Rising. But the news of his activities among the Jacobites, which have caused him to overstay his authorized leave, brings a written reprimand from his commanding officer. Indignant at the unwarranted suspicions of his honor, he first begins to contemplate a shift of loyalties. Yet his doubts are considerable.

> Reason asked, was it worth while to disturb a government so long settled and established, and to plunge a kingdom into all the miseries of

civil war, to replace upon the throne the descendants of a monarch by whom it had been wilfully forfeited. If, on the other hand, his own final conviction of the goodness of their cause, of the commands of his father or uncle, should recommend to him allegiance to the Stuarts, still it was necessary to clear his own character by shewing that he had taken no step to this purpose, as seemed to be falsely insinuated, during his holding the commission of the reigning monarch. (141)

Thus Waverley entertains the question of loyalties that plagued Wallenstein a century earlier, but at this point he reaches a different conclusion.

As he makes his way back toward Edinburgh to proclaim his innocence, he is arrested on suspicion of treason and tried by a magistrate (chaps. 31–32) who manages to cast a negative light on even the most innocuous circumstances surrounding the politically naive Edward. Waverley now finds himself, as a result of his procrastinations, in a position precisely analogous to that of Wallenstein. "Had I yielded to the first generous impulse of indignation, when I learned that my honour was practised upon, how different had been my present situation! I had then been free and in arms, fighting, like my forefathers, for love, for loyalty, and for fame" (166). Even now, however, he is unable to make up his mind and continues to vacillate—between king and Pretender as well as between Rose and Flora.

Rescued from his Hanoverian arrest by Highland renegades, he still wavers between alternatives. Considering himself by his rigorous treatment to have been absolved from any allegiance to the existing government, he debates between a return to the Highlands or a flight to England. Finally matters are taken out of his hands before he has reached any decision. He is presented personally to the Pretender, who in shrewd political calculation offers him a commission in the army of insurgent Jacobites in return for the Hanoverian captaincy from which he has been expelled. Waverley declines a rank because he is unable to raise enough men for a command, but he readily agrees to serve as a volunteer in Fergus's troop of Highlanders. Yet on the eve of the great Battle of Prestonpans, looking down at the tartan in which he is so newly clad, he seems to himself still to be caught in a horrible and unnatural dream. "'Good God,' he thought, 'am I then a traitor to my country, a renegade to my standard, and a foe, as that poor dying wretch expressed himself, to my native England!'" (221). Unlike Wallenstein, however, Waverley is given the opportunity to recover from the traitorous commitment into which he has been forced by circumstances.

After defeating General Cope's army on September 21 at Prestonpans, the Jacobites fail to capitalize immediately on their success and tarry in Edinburgh for several weeks before carrying their campaign southward into England. Initially victorious at Carlisle, the Scottish leaders nevertheless decide in early December to turn back at Derby. During this retreat Waverley gets cut off from the Jacobite forces and must spend several weeks hiding from the advancing English troops in the cottage of a friendly farmer. And now, for the first time, he has the occasion to reflect in tranquillity on his predicament. It was here "that he acquired a more complete mastery of a spirit tamed by adversity, than his former experience had given him; and that he felt himself entitled to say firmly, though perhaps with a sigh, that the romance of his life was ended, and that its real history had now commenced" (283). In other words, he awakens finally from the romantic dream of Jacobitism, a dream that has no place in the new world of reason and common sense.[15]

Now that Waverley has reached this stage of intellectual and emotional maturity, the novel moves rapidly to its conclusion. In April 1746 the Jacobites are decisively defeated at Culloden—an event that is simply reported in the novel, not depicted—, and following this final Jacobite Rising, English rule is firmly reestablished in Scotland. Along with many other rebels, Fergus is captured and executed; Flora flees to France. Once the innocence of his behavior is ascertained, Waverley is pardoned and restored to full honor. Returning to Tully-Veolan, he discovers that both Bradwardine and Rose are safe and alive. Waverley asks for Rose's hand in marriage, and the young couple, with the combined fortunes and fame of two great families of North and South, settles down for life on the Lowland estate—a symbolic compromise that marks Waverley's typical avoidance of extremes and Scott's hope for an eventual synthesis of the two cultures. The new hero, though thrust by circumstances into decisions resembling those faced by Wallenstein and Max, avoids their extremes: he neither accepts his treason, like Wallenstein, nor avoids the dilemma by rushing to his own death, like Max. But precisely this willingness to compromise prevents Waverley from being a "hero" in the fashion that we have observed in all our earlier examples—heroes who, despite their hesitations, were forced ultimately to slay the enemy, kill the mother, ask the question, stab the king, or seek their own deaths. Instead, Scott's new hero seeks a "middle way" between extremes,[16] a synthesizing middle way, according to the conservative Scott, that should take place by evolution, not revolution.

THE HEGELIAN VIEW

The movement of Scott's novel constitutes with considerable precision a fictional analogy to the theory of history that Hegel developed a few years later in his lectures at the University of Berlin.[17] Hegel's scheme, as outlined in the introduction to his lectures, was that history, in its grand movement from East to West, progresses through the conflict of opposing forces—not nations but *principles*—a process that results in a synthesis, which in turn becomes the basis for a new opposition—and so forth ad infinitum until, in the final synthesis, the oppositions of church and state in Europe disappear in a final ideal society.[18] Scott, with no possible awareness of the direction of Hegel's thought, advanced a similar idea in the postscript to *Waverley* (chap. 72), where he asserted that no European nation in the course of a half century had undergone such a total transformation as Scotland.

> The effects of the insurrection of 1745,—the destruction of the patriarchal power of the Highland chiefs,—the abolition of the heritable jurisdictions of the Lowland nobility and barons,—the total eradication of the Jacobite party, which, averse to intermingle with the English, or adopt their customs, long continued to pride themselves upon maintaining ancient Scottish manners and customs, commenced this innovation. The gradual influx of wealth, and extension of commerce, have since united to render the present people of Scotland a class of beings as different from their grandfathers, as the existing English are from those of Queen Elizabeth's time. (340)

These vast changes, he continues, though steady and progressive, have been gradual. "Like those who drift down the stream of a deep and smooth river, we are not aware of the progress we have made until we fix our eye on the now distant point from which we set out." Accordingly, his novel recording great events "Sixty Years Since" looks back at the past from a present that, while different, has also absorbed into its own culture the results of those changes. As Lukács has noted, Scott's historical perspective is achieved not by alluding in his narrative to present events; instead he "brings the past to life as the prehistory of the present."[19] But his awareness of the historical necessity of the past to give way, even in its most beloved aspects, is utterly Hegelian.

Scott's sense of historical perspective is evident throughout the novel, and the phrase "sixty years since" echoes as a leitmotif whenever the author wants to stress the difference between the reader's present and the conditions about 1745: when Waverley's Aunt Rachel, for example, gives him a purse of gold pieces, "which also were more common Sixty Years since than they have been of late" (30). Or with respect to Colonel Talbot's harsh attitude toward the condemned Fergus: "Let us devoutly hope, that, in this respect at least, we shall never see the scenes, or hold the sentiments, that were general in Britain Sixty Years since" (319).

England and Scotland had seen vast changes during the later eighteenth and early nineteenth centuries, changes more striking and rapid than in any other country of Europe.[20] England, whose national economy was the first in the world to be fully industrialized, was almost a century ahead of Germany and most other European nations in experiencing the Industrial Revolution. Industrialization brought with it such modern features as the urbanization and commercialization of society, the centralization of government, and the capitalist economy that forever changed the landscape and culture of the country—changes well remarked by Blake, Wordsworth, Carlyle, and other writers of the period. In the wake of the French Revolution, startling new views on social and political affairs streamed inexorably across the Channel, and the accompanying rise of the bourgeoisie brought growing demands for democratization. Even the nature of war changed irremediably with the mass armies of the Napoleonic campaigns.

Hegel first recognized the implications of these changes for literature—for the classical forms of epic and drama as well as traditional ideas regarding heroism—and incorporated them into his lectures on aesthetics. For Hegel, the heroic age was the time represented in the Homeric epics, in which the basis for all action was virtue (*aretê*) in a community where individual and group shared a common ethic.[21] He contrasts that "heroic age" with the "present prosaic conditions" (1:192–94), in which the realm for ideal action is limited and in which independent application of shared ethical values has given way to subjective attitudes or beliefs ("Gesinnungen"). The monarchs of our time no longer resemble the dominating heroes of the mythic age, who embodied the values of their people and created new nations; instead, they represent simply a more or less abstract focal point within existing institutions determined by laws and constitutions. Similarly, while military leaders may still enjoy considerable power, the goals and interests are assigned to them and the realm for personal decision is quite narrow. (Thus the Swiss dramatist Friedrich Dürrenmatt sardonically observed that nowadays "Creon's secretaries would deal with the case of Antigone.")[22]

In his subsequent discussion of epic poetry (2:412–23) Hegel refers to his explication of the heroic age, asking what kind of general world-state must exist if an epic event is to achieve an appropriate representation within it. Citing the total unity of individual and community in the conception of right and equity and ethics in the heroic age, he goes on to assert that "a situation of state with an already organized constitution, with fully developed laws, with a thoroughgoing jurisdiction, well established administration, ministries, state chancelleries, police, and so forth—must be excluded as the basis for any genuinely epic action." In the heroic age, man was at one with his surroundings. He himself created everything that he required for living, fighting, traveling, cooking, eating, and drinking. Nothing had as yet become a mere dead means to an end. "Our present-day machine and factory society," in contrast, "along with the products that emerge from it as well as the manner of satisfying our external needs for living, would be just as inadequate as modern state organization for a life background required by the original epic."

Hegel's view is close to the argument advanced by Thomas Carlyle in his lectures titled *Heroes, Hero-Worship and the Heroic in History* (1841). The last of Carlyle's six classes of hero—after the hero as divinity, prophet, poet, priest, and man of letters—is the hero as king, whom Carlyle regards as "the most important of great men" and "the summary for us of *all* the various figures of heroism."[23] For Carlyle, it is "the world's sad predicament in these times of ours" that they are times of revolution, an unbelieving century that has lost its faith in heroes. The "forgeries" brought forth in such times of disorder and chaos have led men to trust nothing. Indeed, the "last great man," writes Carlyle in 1840, was Napoleon. But the "fatal charlatan-element" in Napoleon prevented him from achieving the greatness of a Cromwell. Under these circumstances, Carlyle is reassured only by the "expressibly precious fact" of hero worship— "the most solacing fact one sees in the world at present" (191).

In sum, modern society itself cannot provide the necessary foundation for epic and heroes as offered by the primordial community. If we apply Hegel's categories to Scott's *Waverley*, we easily see that the clan community represented by Fergus and Flora still provides such a heroic life-style, and it brings forth the kind of heroic poetry chanted by Flora against the background of the wild Scottish Highlands. But that primitive community, Scott implies with bittersweet nostalgia, is destined to give way to a modern society in which the hero is the man resourceful enough to find compromises among the conflicting alternatives offered in a rapidly changing world. The German philosopher and the Scottish novelist, each in his own way, acknowledged the unrelenting power of history and the inevitability of change—even at the expense of cherished ideals of ethics and heroism. In this new world, which condemns such primal heroes as Fergus Mac-Ivor, the wavering Waverley emerges as the representative "hero" of the day. The moment of hesitation becomes a permanent mode of life.

ROMANTIC VARIETIES

It is an oversimplification to assert, as Sean O'Faolain has done in the title of his book, that the hero simply "vanishes" in the course of the past two centuries or, according to Mario Praz, goes "into eclipse."[24] O'Faolain can make his argument only because he offers a narrower conception of the heroic than we have been following. We can readily agree with his premises—that "the Hero is a purely social creation" and that "most of our traditional certainties have become progressively less and less certain" (16). But his conclusion—that the hero is "a personification of those certainties"—is much less plausible. For we have seen that many heroes from antiquity down to the end of the eighteenth century are interesting and tragic precisely because they are forced to question those "traditional certainties." Similarly, Praz can make his argument—that in the democratic art of the novel, which lacks heroes and heroines, attention becomes concentrated on the details of common life (375)—only by focusing, as he does, on Dickens, Thackeray, Trollope, and Eliot. It is more accurate, I believe, to say that an increasingly fragmented society has produced a variety of heroes to suit its needs.

Literature of the later nineteenth and twentieth centuries had its heroes, of course. The titular hero of Joseph Conrad's *Lord Jim* (1900), for instance, possesses all the qualities of a conventional hero. "The conquest of love, honour, men's confidence—the pride of it, the power of it, are fit materials for a heroic tale," his narrator Marlow observes midway through his account (chap. 22). In the eyes of his Malayan admirers in remote Patusan, "Tuan Jim" is surrounded by legends and by the superstitious belief that, like Wallenstein, he is invulnerable; and like Aeneas he establishes a safe new community in the foreign land where he arrives. But in 1900, when Conrad published his masterpiece, it was necessary to send his figures, like Kurtz, into the heart of darkness and to leave behind "this world of doubts" (chap. 23) in order for them to achieve heroic stature. What his heroes confront is not the clash of cultures, but their own existential doubts—in Lord Jim's case, the concerns about his personal courage and honor. Jim, who "goes away from a living woman to celebrate his pitiless wedding with a shadowy ideal of conduct" (chap. 45), finally is much more like Max Piccolomini than Wallenstein. Repeatedly termed a "romantic" by Marlow and his friend Stein, he suffers no doubts, no hesitation, as he crosses the river to his certain self-sacrificing death at the end of the novel.

By the same token, the titular hero of Melville's *Billy Budd* (written in the 1890s, published in 1924) is a hero admired by his mates and eternalized in sailors' myths. But, like Lord Jim, he is an unproblematic and naive youth whose heroism must be sought in the isolation of a British warship, far from the customs and beliefs of contemporary (1797) England. His "hesitation" before he strikes the blow that kills his tormenter Claggart, does not stem from any conflict of values but from frustration at the stutter that afflicts him in moments of stress and prevents him from expressing in words his outrage at Claggart's insult to his honor. The figure suffering a truly heroic conflict of values is Captain Vere, who is torn not only between his paternal affection for Billy and his contempt for his first-mate Claggart but also, in a period of naval mutiny, between the perceived need for drumhead justice to maintain order and the option of delaying the trial until his ship can rejoin the main fleet.

Another distinct variety, labeled variously the "unheroic hero" or the "sick hero," has been widely proposed as typical of French literature.[25] Afflicted by "excessive individualism, acute self-consciousness, and neurotic introspection," these Romantic heroes are invariably young—in their teens or twenties—and characterized by their intelligence, sensitivity, and insight.[26] The enormous popularity of books featuring such self-centered and often lethargic "heroes"—Stendhal's Julien Sorel and Fabrice del Dongo or Flaubert's Frédéric Moreau, for example—has been attributed to a variety of social, political, and religious factors that frustrated a generation coming to maturity during the disruptions of the Napoleonic era.[27]

While Pasco's definition of romanticism—featuring insecurity, escapism, depression—does not apply to early German and English literature of the period (or, as we have seen, to Scott),[28] such a hero radicalized almost to the point of caricature is represented by the central figure in the five related stories that Lermontov published under the title *A Hero of Our Own Times* (1840).[29] A lost soul in his own eyes as well as the eyes of others—corrupt, immoral, sadistic, contemptuous, bitter, spiteful, crafty, pitiless, willful—Pechorin is presented by Lermontov in his author's introduction as a portrait of his age. "My hero embodies the vices of our whole generation in the full flush of development" (xviii). Wealthy by birth, he indulged as a young man in all the pleasures that money can buy, in the life of the fashionable world, in love affairs with society beauties, in studies and the sciences—only to be bored by it all (57). After his mind has been thus corrupted by the world, he finds only one expedient still left to him—travel and adventure (58). Journeying to the Caucasus at age twenty-five as an officer, he dies only five years later, having in the interval had a brief marriage with a Circassian beauty, killed a friend in an unnecessary duel, and betrayed a Russian princess for reasons of sheer self-interest. Even in death he remains totally self-centered. "When I contemplate the imminence of death, I think only of myself" (238). Yet Lermontov portrays many of the people surrounding Pechorin in tones hardly less cynical, representing a society of which his "hero" may truly be called typical. "We are no longer capable of great sacrifices for the welfare of mankind," Pechorin writes in his diary,

> or even for our own personal happiness, since we know happiness to be unattainable. We pass therefore from doubt to doubt, as our ancestors passed from delusion to delusion, but, unlike them, we are devoid of hope, lacking even the undefinable but vivid pleasure which fills the minds of those who struggle against their fellows or against fate. (275–76)

But "heroes" of this sort, even though presented as typical of their age, whether in Russia or France, cannot embody any grand conflicts within their culture because their concerns, and those of their age, are so utterly subjective, self-centered, and selfish. They may exemplify the disintegration and decline of a culture, but no conflict of values within it.

We see the dead end to which this attitude leads in the forty-year-old narrator of Dostoyevsky's *Notes from Underground* (1864), who has retired from his menial government position and retreated to a shabby room on the outskirts of town, where he does nothing but think and record the turn of events that led to his present state of boredom, resentment, and inertia. Even if he wanted to take revenge for the insults he has suffered, "I should probably find it impossible to make up my mind to take any steps, even if I could" (20).[30] For he has convinced himself that "every kind of intellectual activity is a disease" (18). If a man is to act, he must be absolutely sure of himself. "No doubts must remain anywhere" (27). But because the nameless Underground Man has no foundations on which to base his convictions, he can only sit and nurture his resentment.

> Reason is a good thing, that can't be disputed, but reason is only reason and satisfies only man's intellectual faculties, while volition is a manifestation of the whole of life, I mean of the whole of human life *including* both reason and speculation. (35)

As a result, he has concluded that it is best to do nothing—to cultivate a "conscious inertia" (43). He sets down the record of his life—that is, certain incidents that occurred when he was twenty-four years old—out of sheer boredom. But the image that emerges from his narrative, he concludes on the last page, is that of what he calls an "antihero": a man who has lost the habit of living and has decayed morally, while "carefully cultivating my anger underground" (122).[31] From the famous heroes of antiquity we have come full circle to the nameless antiheroes who populate the modern world.

MODERN MODIFICATIONS

The wavering hero continued to fulfill the expectations of an age whose ideas of settled values had been ruthlessly overturned by the Napoleonic era and that was now at sea in a world of competing claims: in his permanent state of vacillation this hero exemplifies tensions at work in the writer's own culture. Scott, to be sure, permitted his readers to bask in a virtually Hegelian confidence that the conflict portrayed in his novel had been resolved and absorbed into his contemporary culture, which was now confronted with new concerns of its own. But no such assurances accompany the wavering hero who is still very much present in our own time. In the twentieth century, instead, writers have appropriated the figure to suit their own purposes and, in every case, to suggest the uncertainty and futility of their age.

Miguel de Unamuno's tragicomic novel *Mist* (1914)—or, as he called it, *nivola*—features a hero, Augusto Pérez, who is so indecisive that he has difficulty on the first page of the story with the simple act of opening his umbrella. The pampered son of a recently deceased mother, he leads a meaningless life conditioned almost entirely by habit and abstract thought and unencumbered by any knowledge of the real world. He stands at the door of his house, wondering which way to go—to the right or to the left. He decides to wait until a dog passes, "and I will start out in the direction that he takes" (22).[32] As it happens, it is not a dog but a beautiful young woman who passes in front of his house, and Augusto's pursuit of her leads into the various complications of the plot. (The young woman, Eugenia, is a piano teacher who dislikes music, and a deceitful schemer who uses Augusto for her own purposes.) At every step he remains indecisive and leaves matters up to chance: he can't make up his mind to enter Eugenia's house, for instance, until her aunt appears on the balcony and drops a canary cage, which Augusto is then able to rescue. He later reports to his dog Orfeo—to whom he addresses many of his most revealing monologues—that he has taken the decisive step by entering her home.

> "Do you know what it is to take a decisive step? The winds of fortune drive us along and all of our steps are decisive. Our steps? But are these steps ours? We are travelling through a wild and tangled forest, Orfeo, in which there are no trails. We make the trails ourselves with our feet as we go along at random. There are persons who think they are following their star; I am following a double star, a twin star. And this star is only the projection of the trail upon the sky—the projection of chance." (71)

When various accidents cause him to fall in love with a second young woman, he consults his friend Victor, who advises him to marry one of them without thinking too much about it.

> "Yes, but—I am assailed by so many doubts."
> "All the better, little Hamlet, all the better! You doubt? Then you think? Then you are."
> "Yes, doubting is thinking."

"And thinking is doubting, and nothing but doubting. One believes, one knows, one imagines, all without doubting. Neither belief,
nor knowledge, nor imagination presupposes doubt. They are even
destroyed by doubt. But one never thinks without doubting." (251)

When Augusto is deceived by both women, in his despair he contemplates suicide. But it occurs to him, first, to go to Salamanca and
consult the philosopher Unamuno, with whose writing, including
an essay on suicide, he was familiar. Unamuno points out to him
that he cannot commit suicide because, after all, he doesn't exist
except as a character of fiction. "'You are only a product of my imagination and of the imagination of those of my readers who read this
story which I have written of your fictitious adventures and misfortunes'" (294). Augusto succeeds in committing suicide by eating
himself to death and then appears to Unamuno in a dream to suggest that perhaps it is Unamuno himself who is the creature of fiction. "It may easily be that you are nothing more than an excuse for
spreading my story through the world, and other stories like mine;
and that presently, when you are dead and gone, it is we who then
keep your soul alive" (322).

Unamuno, who noted wryly that his novel *Mist* had enjoyed much
greater international acclaim than his major philosophical work,
The Tragic Sense of Life (1913), has adopted the by now familiar figure of the hesitant hero to exemplify his philosophical ideas. What
defines humanity is the consciousness lacking in the world of nature. Yet inherent in that consciousness is, for Unamuno, the
tragedy of life. Like Dostoyevsky's Underground Man, to whom he
felt spiritually akin, Unamuno begins with the premise that "consciousness is a disease." Living and knowing are such antinomies
that "everything vital is, not only irrational, but anti-rational, and
everything rational is anti-vital." Augusto's thinking incapacitates
him for any decisions—even such simple ones as which way to turn
for his daily walk. But his indecisiveness, so humorously depicted in
the novel, reflects a larger uncertainty about life altogether and the
relationship of life to thought.

In his reflections on *Our Lord Don Quixote* (1905), Unamuno had
claimed that although we sometimes regard writers as real persons

and view the characters they invent as purely imaginary, the truth is exactly the reverse. "The characters are real, it is they who are the authentic beings, and they make use of the person who seems to be of flesh and blood in order to assume form and being in the eyes of men."[33] Unamuno makes the serious claim that Don Quixote and Sancho Panza have more historical reality than Cervantes himself, and that "far from Cervantes being their creator, it is they who created Cervantes" (430). In *Mist* he puts this theory into action. But it is precisely this implicit reference to the uncertainty of our own world as well as the possible fictitiousness of our own existence that produces the ambiguous effect of weird amusement and existential anxiety with which we read Unamuno's novel.[34]

If Unamuno used the type of the hesitant hero as a vehicle for his ideas on existence and the frangibility of human nature, in a novel written that same year Franz Kafka adapted the same figure to set forth his ideas on ethics. *The Trial* (written in 1914–15, published in 1925) is a book about guilt and responsibility: the inevitability of man's guilt in the world and man's freedom to accept the responsibility for his own guilt.[35] Guilt and freedom are inextricably intertwined. To be free means, for Kafka, to recognize and accept the fact of one's guilt. There is no innocence—only the freedom of the man who recognizes and accepts his guilt. Kafka expressed this idea most succinctly in a cryptic note from the sketch "He," in which he asserted that "original sin, the ancient wrong that man has committed, consists in the reproach that man makes and from which he never desists: that a wrong has been done unto him and that original sin has been committed against him."[36] Like most of Kafka's paradoxes, this one defies everyday logic, but it explains Josef K.'s predicament. He is guilty from the moment he wakes up on the first page of *The Trial* to find himself arrested—because, as he immediately protests, he has been falsely accused. (It never occurs to him to admit that he is actually guilty of the various existential "crimes" that become evident in the course of the narrative.) His sin, in the words of the paradox, resides in his insistence that an injustice has been done unto him. The paradox has a further implication. Man is redeemed in the instant that he accepts the responsibility for his guilt, rather than feeling that he is being wrongly accused by a hostile world. But most men refuse to accept this freedom. Instead they attempt, by what Kafka calls a process of *motivation,* to project their guilt onto the world outside and thereby to deny it.[37]

These ideas underlie the plot of *The Trial* and account for its action and Josef K.'s constant hesitations. Since K. is unwilling to accept the responsibility for his guilt and to approach the Law directly, he constantly delays and hesitates by seeking helpers to aid him in his case. He surrounds himself with a variety of mediating figures, who stand, as it were, between him and his responsibility. Initially he even avoids the assistance of the men who might be in a position to help him and, instead, appeals to peripheral women: Fräulein Bürstner, who lives in the same house, for the remote reason that she is soon to become a secretary in a legal office; the wife of the court usher; Leni, the maid of the lawyer Huld; and finally the artist Titorelli, who paints portraits of the court officials.

The novel, though incomplete, has a clear beginning and end: it begins when K. wakes up one morning to find himself accused by the court; and it ends exactly a year later when he is taken out and executed. The time in between is filled—there is no development—by a series of static repetitions as K. seeks ever new ways of staving off the inevitable, and liberating, acknowledgment of guilt. But in Kafka's world there is no decision among clear alternatives— only constant uncertainty. His situation is symbolized close to the end by the parable concerning the man from the country who begs admittance to the Law but, instead of entering, sits waiting for days and years, unsuccessfully importuning the doorkeeper to let him in. When he finally dies, he learns from the doorkeeper that this door was meant for him alone and will now be closed.

Even in the moment of his own death K. remains indecisive. Led out of town by his two executioners, he continues to look around desperately for a savior or rescuer. As his executioners pass the butcher knife back and forth over his head, he realizes that he is expected to seize the knife and plunge it into his own breast. But even now he is unable to make the decision that would have represented the acceptance of his guilt. "He could not completely rise to the occasion, he could not relieve the officials of all their tasks; the responsibility for this last failure of his lay with him who had not left him the remnant of strength necessary for the deed."[38] His last thoughts, as they thrust the knife into his heart, are indecisive questions about yet another possible helper he suddenly glimpses at a distance in a window. "Who was it? A friend? A good man? Someone who sympathized? Someone who wanted to help? Was it one person only? Or was it mankind? Was help at hand?"

Scott initiated the career of the wavering hero in 1814, at the end of the Napoleonic Wars which destroyed the last vestiges of feudal absolutism with its traditional heroes and inaugurated the rise of the modern middle class. Exactly a hundred years later, on the eve of the Great War that shattered all the imagined certainties of that nineteenth-century bourgeois society, troubled writers such as Unamuno and Kafka resurrected that same wavering hero for their modern fictions. But now he wavers in a world of uncertainties with no hope of resolution. For his uncertainties do not stem, as earlier, from the simple conflict of two opposing ideologies, but from the perceived frangibility of existence itself and the ethical consciousness of universal guilt. And his authors offer no hope that his uncertainties will be resolved in a great Hegelian synthesis.[39]

Conclusion: Continuities

As I proposed in the introduction, I have not sought to produce here an all-embracing typology of the hero or to generate a grand theory of the heroic. From Aeneas, who hesitates momentarily before plunging his sword into Turnus's chest, to Josef K., whose year-long pattern of temporization finally compels his executioners to thrust their butcher knife into his heart, we have witnessed a transformation of the hero almost to the point of total inversion. Working inductively from the psychologically motivated hesitations and delays of those figures, we examined the manner in which moments of personal inhibition can unmask deep-lying cultural crises in the fictions within which the heroes exist as well as in the writers' own society.

What have the vacillations of these heroes exposed? From Aeneas and Orestes by way of Parzival and Hamlet down to Wallenstein, the hesitation revealed from case to case a classic opposition of binary forces. This opposition represented no difficulty for such traditional heroes as Achilles or Beowulf, who unequivocally embodied one side of the equation. But heroes emerging at later stages of their respective cultures were faced with a choice. What I have labeled the "Trojan dilemma" (see Chapter 2) compelled Aeneas and Orestes to choose between the ancient code of blood vengeance and the new civic virtues of compassion, mercy, law, and justice. For Aeneas, who underwent his formative years before the symbolic turning point of the Trojan War, this dilemma led to a brief reversion from the inhibitions of the Roman ideal, proclaimed by his father and toward which he was striving, to the savage lust to avenge his young friend Pallas. Orestes, in contrast, had different experiences: both post-Trojan and Delphic/Phocian (that is, somewhat outside the sphere of influence that conditioned Agamemnon and the other primitive Greek heroes). His deed of blood vengeance against his mother was motivated by divine command and not by any primal urge. In both cases the hesitations marked turning points in the history of their respective peoples: a final eruption of the primitive before the triumph of civilization—a civilization maintained, however, only by the watchful repression of aggressive impulses that could burst forth again at any moment. More than a thousand years later Parzival confronted mutatis mutandis an equally radical opposition: between the claims of religion and knighthood, or church and court. Inhibited initially by the restrictive rules of courtly behavior, which caused him to forgo the compassionate question, he succeeded through birthright and heroism in reconciling the two spheres in an ideal realm that had no counterpart in everyday medieval reality. Hamlet began, as the language of the play makes clear, in a rational world of binary opposites, but the intrusion of the irrational through the apparition of the ghost evokes an existential anxiety that causes his delays and hesitations and inhibits any action. The final catastrophe is not initiated by Hamlet; he is a victim of it. Wallenstein, too, is caught between opposing forces: Catholic and Protestant, South and North, Austria and Sweden; he is gradually forced to the quintessentially modern recognition of his own powerlessness in the face of political factors that he had believed he could control with playful skill.

In all these cases the inhibitions and hesitations of heroes projected into earlier eras reflect, as Freud proposed, tensions that the writers observed in their own societies. Virgil and Aeschylus used their heroes as vehicles through which to analogize the violence and lawlessness that they sensed, seething and barely controlled, just beneath the surface in Rome and Athens as these respective cultures moved through war and civil strife toward constitutional societies of law. Wolfram turned to Celtic myth to express his dismay at the conflict between emperor and pope in early thirteenth-century Germany and to project his vision of an ideal (Hegelian *avant la lettre,* if you will) synthesis of the two opposing powers. Hamlet's hesitation reflected the anomy with which Shakespeare and many of his contemporaries saw England afflicted in a period of philosophical skepticism, legal controversy, and religious strife. Finally, Schiller held up the Thirty Years' War as a warning example against the dangers facing Europe in the years following the French Revolution.

Waverley's wavering, like Wallenstein's delaying tactics, exposed the political, religious, social, and cultural turmoil unsettling the still uncertain Union of England and Scotland. But with Waverley we leave the realm of heroes in the traditional as well as Hegelian sense and observe a nonheroic central figure who is little more than the plaything of these conflicts without affecting them in the least. Like the earlier heroes, Waverley belongs to the past, but his world foreshadows the controversies of Scott's own England and Scotland during the social upheaval of revolutions both political and industrial. Through his actions, or non-actions, he initiates a series of nineteenth-century nonheroes whose wavering reflects no conflict *within* the society but, instead, their own alienation *from* the society. In contrast to their hesitating predecessors, who sooner or later act, these lethargic waverers almost invariably belong to the writer's own time. From the French "sick heroes" to the Russian "antiheroes," these figures are virtually incapacitated by their intelligence and critical thinking, and amount to voluntary exiles, whether in the Caucasus or in the spiritual underground of their own lonely rooms. When these figures do in fact display "heroic" characteristics and deeds, each must flee his society with its restrictive rules and laws to seek exotic and remote retreats: Lord Jim's Pacific islands or Billy Budd's British warship. In the early twentieth-century, finally, inhibition and hesitation became virtually a modus vivendi for such figures as Augusto Pérez and Josef K., whose only "action" amounts to the suicide (or self-imposed murder) that finally liberates them from the uncertainties and responsibilities of a modern world with which they are unable to cope.

We have seen heroes who are experienced leaders and warriors like Aeneas and Wallenstein, and youths forced by external circumstances into action, or at least maturity: Orestes, Parzival, Hamlet, and Waverley. While invariably intelligent, the early heroes are rarely intellectuals: the university-educated Hamlet is the first, and the succession of intellectual heroes from French romanticism by way of the Underground Man to Augusto Pérez suggests that deliberation is more of a hindrance to heroic action than a help. One cynical and melancholy message of these various poetic fictions would appear to be that heroism and intellectuality rarely go hand in hand—that the *vita activa* and the *vita contemplativa* are mutually exclusive.

The transformation of the hesitant hero into the wavering one was accompanied by a corresponding change in literary form. "Is Achilles possible side by side with powder and lead?" Marx asked in his "Introduction to the Critique of Political Economy" (written 1857).

> Or is the Iliad at all compatible with the printing press and steam press? Do not singing and reciting and the muses necessarily go out of existence with the appearance of the printer's bar, and do not, therefore, the prerequisites of epic poetry disappear?[1]

The epic, and increasingly the drama, offered themselves for centuries as the appropriate genres in which the dilemmas of heroes torn between simple oppositions could be portrayed—usually in a poetic language sufficiently mysterious to suggest complexities of meaning that could not be fully accommodated in words. But as the clear oppositions of antiquity and feudalism began to give way to the more generalized anxieties prevailing in the modern industrialized, urbanized, and commercialized world, the classical forms also yielded to the typically modern and freer form of the novel. In the novel the "hero" is no longer required to be heroic; he can justify his role simply as the focal point of multiple fictional energies.

The transformations of the hero in literature, of course, imply no corresponding decline of bravery in our world. The actions of the New York firefighters on September 11, 2001, who rushed into the conflagration of the World Trade Center in the effort to rescue their fellow citizens, provide stirring evidence to the contrary. But heroism in the traditional or Hegelian sense implies more than bravery. (The distinction is analogous to the one, for example, between purist-academic and more popular-colloquial definitions of the terms "tragedy" and "tragic.")[2] Our society has brought forth a few "heroes" whose actions exemplify the collective values of their people and thereby become foundational: Mahatma Gandhi, Martin Luther King, and Nelson Mandela, for example. These recent "world-historical individuals" (in Hegel's term) have not been subject to the internal conflicts of our hesitant heroes. Like Achilles or Beowulf, they have been driven by powerful convictions regarding a world sharply polarized into realms perceived as good and evil: freedom versus oppression (in its various manifestations as colonialism, segregation, or apartheid). Such binary oppositions, which typically play on underlying religious convictions, have provided their followers with reassuring certainties of a virtually primal validity in the face of the entangled and often threatening webs that characterize the modern technological and globalized world. Indeed, successful political leaders have most often been those who are able to reduce historical complexities to the simple slogans of a Manichaean world view and who attract their followers through a policy of opposition.

Popular fiction, films, and video games teem with "action heroes" who save the world from the villains of the decade. These transmogrifications of the traditional hero are presented to us in contemporary equivalents of Homeric epic or Shakespearean drama: large-screen entertainments featuring overscale figures with no moral scruples—Superman or James Bond or Rambo—with whom few viewers in their rational moments can possibly identify. The popularity of fantasy fiction and films—*Star Wars, The Lord of the Rings,* or *The Matrix,* for example—which take place in remote times and places where the clash between good and evil can be portrayed as clear and vivid, is likewise a symptom of our nostalgia for heroes in a world of simple dichotomies. Yet while we may long for the certainties of Achilles and Beowulf or their contemporary equivalents, is it not because we in our modern world are afflicted with the doubts of those culturally more sophisticated heroes from Aeneas to Wallenstein? How many of us living in our multicultural, diversified, and relativized societies are still convinced that universally accepted moral absolutes are possible? Do thinking individuals still confidently believe that we fully control our destinies, or do we regard ourselves as playthings of the gods—even if today's gods bear the names of global conglomerates or the impersonal faces of big government?

If we can give any credence to the analysis of the poets—if literature holds up a true mirror to the world and is not simply the distorted self-reflection of troubled writers—then a certain indecisiveness has become endemic in our society and accordingly in the literary figures in whom many of us—like the reader in whom Baudelaire saw "Hypocrite lecteur, —mon semblable, —mon frère!"—have willy-nilly recognized ourselves. The characters from Waverley to Woody Allen, whom even their creators only ironically termed "heroes" and whom the twentieth century nevertheless came to regard as archetypal, were no longer Aeneases or Parzivals or even Wallensteins. Instead, they were figures in whom hesitation had become absolute: T. S. Eliot's J. Alfred Prufrock, "politic, cautious, and meticulous," who disclaims any similarity to Prince Hamlet and has "time yet for a hundred indecisions"; Franz Kafka's Josef K., who steadfastly refuses to make any decision about his responsibility for his own actions; or Samuel Beckett's Vladimir and Estragon, who seek simply to endure the existential boredom of waiting for Godot. This process was perhaps inevitable in a world grown so complex that the individual has come to feel increasingly helpless and marginalized—in a society so diversified that its "heroes," in reality as well as in literature, have appeared more often than not to achieve identity through difference, alienation, and opposition rather than through exemplarity. Does the word "hero" even occur in the discourse of identity politics? in a digitized world of PINs, passwords, and number sequences on the multiple cards with which we must daily certify various aspects of our identities?

Having reached that point of stasis, can the hero recover? It remains to be seen what transformations of the hero, and of the heroine, the postmodern millennium will bring forth. After Hegel and Marx, is a modern Achilles or Aeneas still conceivable? Or has our globalized world become so diffuse—socially, culturally, financially, ethnically, religiously—that we can produce bosses but no Beowulf, parliamentarians but no Parzivals? Every age gets the heroes and heroines it deserves. Will the literature of the future feature epics of inspired Davids exhorting their followers in a religious exaltation to assail opponents denounced as evil? Dramas of wavering corporate Orestes being goaded into action by their whistle-blowing Electras?[3] Or poetic meditations of indecisive thinkers incapable of moving beyond thought to action? Whatever form our fictions may take and whatever themes they may embody: if we look beyond the psychology of the characters to the cultural myths that engender and sustain them, the "heroes" and "heroines" we imagine can inevitably be read as the projection of each age's endeavor to confront humanity's collective dreads and dreams.

Notes

Introduction

1. Roger Smith, *Inhibition: History and Meaning of the Sciences of Mind and Brain* (London: Free Association Books, 1992), 226.

2. Joseph Campbell, *The Hero with a Thousand Faces* (Princeton: Princeton University Press, 1949); C. M. Bowra, *Heroic Poetry* (New York: St. Martin's, 1961); Gilbert Murray, *Hamlet and Orestes* (New York: Oxford University Press, 1914).

3. I am indebted to Eric Ziolkowski for this reference.

4. Max Weber, "Wissenschaft als Beruf," in his *Schriften zur Wissenschaftslehre*, ed. Michael Sukale (Stuttgart: Reclam, 1991), 237–73; here 244.

1. Aeneas

1. Nicholas Horsfall, in *A Companion to the Study of Virgil*, ed. Nicholas Horsfall (Leiden: Brill, 1995), 192n2, mentions over 130 books and articles devoted to *Aeneid* 12. I cite Virgil's works according to the text in the Loeb Classical Library edition: *Virgil*, ed. H. Rushton Fairclough, rev. ed., 2 vols. (Cambridge: Harvard University Press, 1969–74).

2. W. R. Johnson, *Darkness Visible: A Study in Vergil's Aeneid* (Berkeley: University of California Press, 1976), 122; see also Michael C. J. Putnam, *Virgil's Aeneid: Interpretation and Influence* (Chapel Hill: University of North Carolina Press, 1995), 87–91.

3. The parallels between the *Aeneid* and Homer's *Iliad* and *Odyssey* have been thoroughly pursued by classical scholars. They are grounded theoretically in the cyclical view of history that Virgil proposes as early as in his fourth *Eclogue* (4. 36), where he prophesies that there will be other wars and that a new Achilles will be sent again against a new Troy ("atque iterum ad Troiam magnus mittetur Achilles").

147

4. Adam Parry, "The Two Voices of Virgil's *Aeneid*," *Arion* 2 (1963): 66–80. On early "bivocalism" see Horsfall's *Aeneid* chapter in *Companion to Virgil*, esp. 192–98.

5. Domenico Comparetti, *Vergil in the Middle Ages*, trans. E. F. M. Benecke (1895; rpt. Princeton: Princeton University Press, 1997), 104–18, esp. 107–11.

6. Heinrich von Veldeke, *Eneasroman. Die Berliner Handschrift mit Übersetzung und Kommentar*, ed. Hans Fromm (Frankfurt am Main: Deutscher Klassiker Verlag, 1992), vv. 13,221 ff.

7. Anna Cox Brinton, Introduction to *Mapheus Vegius and His Thirteenth Book of the Aeneid: A Chapter on Virgil in the Renaissance* (Stanford: Stanford University Press, 1930), 1–2 and 33–40.

8. Brinton, *Mapheus Vegius*, 30; Brant's woodcuts are reproduced in Brinton *passim*. On Vegius see also Richard F. Thomas, *Virgil and the Augustan Reception* (Cambridge: Cambridge University Press, 2001), 279–84.

9. Brinton, *Mapheus Vegius*, 54.

10. Ibid., 90.

11. The following examples from Lauren Scancarelli Seem, "The Limits of Chivalry: Tasso and the End of the *Aeneid*," *Comparative Literature* 42 (1990): 116–25.

12. For a discussion of further examples—Ariosto's *Orlando Furioso*, Spenser's *Faerie Queen*, and Milton's *Paradise Lost*—see James Lawrence Shulman, *The Pale Cast of Thought: Hesitation and Decision in the Renaissance Epic* (Newark: University of Delaware Press, 1998).

13. See, for instance, the chapter on Dryden in Thomas, *Augustan Reception*, 122–53.

14. Theodore Ziolkowski, *Virgil and the Moderns* (Princeton: Princeton University Press, 1993), 178–81.

15. Ibid., 163–78.

16. Ibid., 119–34; here 133.

17. Ibid., 48–52.

18. For a representative selection of these works see *Wege zu Vergil. Drei Jahrzehnte Begegnungen in Dichtung und Wissenschaft*, ed. Hans Oppermann (Darmstadt: Wissenschaftliche Buchgesellschaft, 1963).

19. Kenneth Quinn, *Virgil's Aeneid: A Critical Description* (Ann Arbor: University of Michigan Press, 1968), 273.

20. Johnson, *Darkness Visible*, 8–9. For a careful characterization and contrast of the two schools see this entire section of his introduction (8–16).

21. That this view represents an oversimplification is made clear by Werner Suerbaum, *Vergils "Aeneis." Epos zwischen Geschichte und Gegenwart* (Stuttgart: Reclam, 1999), 347–48, who reminds us that postwar critics in Germany began to recognize the tragic aspects of the vanquished Turnus.

22. Thomas, *Augustan Reception*, esp. Prologue and 278–96.

23. *Servii Grammatici qui feruntur in Vergilii carmina commentarii*, ed. Georg Thilo and Hermann Hagen, vol. 2 (Leipzig: Teubner, 1884), 649: "CUNCTANTEM FLECTERE SERMO COEPERAT omnis intentio ad Aeneae pertinet gloriam: nam et ex eo quod hosti cogitat parcere, pius ostenditur, et ex eo quod eum interimit, pietatis gestat insigne: nam Euandri intuitu Pallantis ulciscitur mortem."

24. Wendell Clausen, *Virgil's Aeneid and the Tradition of Hellenistic Poetry* (Berkeley: University of California Press, 1987), 99.

25. Putnam, *Virgil's Aeneid*, 166.

26. Thomas, *Virgil and the Augustan Reception*, 291.

27. Suerbaum, *Vergils "Aeneis,"* 347 ("Die Schlußszene der *Aeneis* als Schlüsselszene").

28. Quinn, *Virgil's Aeneid*, 274; Putnam, *Virgil's Aeneid*, 4–5; and Suerbaum, *Vergils "Aeneis,"* 349–52.

29. For a detailed characterization of Turnus see Clausen, *Virgil's Aeneid*, 83–90.

30. For a full discussion of the struggle between East and West, as implicit in the ekphrasis of Aeneas's shield, see David Quint, *Epic and Empire: Politics and Generic Form from Virgil to Milton* (Princeton: Princeton University Press, 1993), 24–31.

31. Oswald Spengler, *Der Untergang des Abendlandes. Umrisse einer Morphologie der Weltgeschichte* (Munich: Beck, 1963), 788 (vol. 2, chap. 3, sec. 2, "Historische Pseudomorphosen").

32. A. J. Boyle, "The Meaning of the Aeneid: A Critical Inquiry. Part I: Empire and the Individual: An Examination of the Aeneid's Major Theme," *Ramus* 1 (1972): 63–90; here 72–74.

33. Putnam, *Virgil's Aeneid*, 56–57, 160–62.

34. Charles Segal, "Dido's Hesitation in *Aeneid* 4," *Classical World* 84 (1990): 1–12.

35. For the following paragraph I am indebted principally to Roger Smith, *Inhibition: History and Meaning in the Sciences of Mind and Brain* (London: Free Association Books, 1992), esp. 1–26.

36. "Die 'kulturelle' Sexualmoral und die moderne Nervosität," in Sigmund Freud, *Das Unbehagen in der Kultur und andere kulturtheoretische Schriften*, ed. Alfred Lorenzer and Bernard Görlich, 7th ed. (Frankfurt am Main: Fischer, 2001), 116.

37. "Zeitgemäßes über Krieg und Tod (I)," in Freud, *Unbehagen in der Kultur*, 143.

38. "Das Unbehagen in der Kultur," in *Unbehagen in der Kultur*, 82. Putnam, *Virgil's Aeneid*, 24–49, discusses the counterpoint of love and death in another context.

39. John Kerrigan, *Revenge Tragedy: Aeschylus to Armageddon* (Oxford: Clarendon, 1996), devotes a few pages to Freud's *Beyond the Pleasure Principle* but does not mention *Civilization and Its Discontents*.

40. R. Deryck Williams, "The *Aeneid*," in *Cambridge History of Classical Literature*, vol. 2/3: *The Age of Augustus*, ed. E. J. Kenney (Cambridge: Cambridge University Press, 1983), 50. Elsewhere (9) Williams points out that the European school early argued that Aeneas's failing as a hero implies a criticism of the archaic Homeric concept of heroism (9).

41. Sigmund Freud, *Die Traumdeutung*, 5th ed. (Leipzig: Deuticke, 1919), vi.

42. Ziolkowski, *Virgil and the Moderns*, 3.

43. Quint, *Epic and Empire*, 61.

44. Quinn, *Virgil's Aeneid*, 276.

45. In Freud, "Zeitgemäßes über Krieg und Tod," 142.

46. R. J. Tarrant, "Poetry and Power: Virgil's Poetry in Contemporary Context," in *Cambridge Companion to Virgil*, ed. Charles Martindale (Cambridge: Cambridge University Press, 1997), 169–87, esp. 18off.

47. Ronald Syme, *The Roman Revolution* (Oxford: Clarendon, 1939; rpt. Oxford Paperback, 1960), 2.

48. Freud, "Warum Krieg," in *Unbehagen in der Kultur*, 165ff.

49. Ingemar König, *Der römische Staat. Teil 1: Die Republik* (Stuttgart: Reclam, 1992), 98–99.

50. Gerhard Binder, *Aeneas und Augustus. Interpretationen zum 8. Buch der Aeneis* (Meisenheim am Glan: Anton Hein, 1971).

51. Werner Eck, *Augustus und seine Zeit*, 2d ed. (Munich: Beck, 2000), 105.

52. Suerbaum, *Vergils "Aeneis,"* 334–36. On Virgil's use of typological analogies to relate the world of the *Aeneid* to Augustan Rome generally see Williams, *"Aeneid,"* 37–43.

53. Williams, *"Aeneid,"* 39.

54. Quinn, *Vergil's Aeneid,* 22, 26–34.

55. See especially Parry, "Two Voices"; and Johnson, *Darkness Visible.*

56. Eck, *Augustus und seine Zeit,* 18–22.

57. Putnam, *Virgil's Aeneid,* 21–26.

58. Arnold J. Toynbee, *A Study of History,* abridgement by D. C. Somervell (New York: Oxford University Press, 1946), 453.

59. James J. O'Hara, *Death and the Optimistic Prophecy in Vergil's Aeneid* (Princeton: Princeton University Press, 1990), 6.

60. Quinn, *Virgil's Aeneid,* 22–24; and Suerbaum, *Vergils "Aeneis,"* 354.

61. Putnam, *Virgil's Aeneid,* 87.

62. Horsfall, *Aeneid* chapter, *Companion to Virgil,* 197, 216.

63. Williams, *"Aeneid,"* 57.

64. Johnson, *Darkness Visible,* 133; and Putnam, *Virgil's Aeneid,* 163–64.

65. Williams, *"Aeneid,"* 39; and Putnam, *Virgil's Aeneid,* 14. See also Quint, *Epic and Empire,* 78, who defines two strategies for overcoming the past: clemency, by forgetting, sees repetition of past evil as regressive; revenge, by undoing, sees in repetition the possibility of mastery.

66. Steele Commager, Introduction to *Virgil: A Collection of Critical Essays* (Englewood Cliffs: Prentice-Hall, 1966), 10.

67. I am not unaware of the significance of the religious factor—the conflict between the humanity of Olympian light and the forces of Junonian darkness—that has been elegantly discussed by such scholars as Johnson, *Darkness Visible,* 141–54; and Williams, *"Aeneid,"* 61–66. For my purposes here, however, the transcendental element is less central than the secular analogy.

2. Orestes

1. In two later works, Euripides' melodramatic adventure plays representing subsequent events, Pylades has greater opportunity to express in words his role as the paragon of loyal friendship. In *Orestes,* he assists his friend in the plot, subsequently thwarted by the gods, to murder Helen of Troy and kidnap her daughter Hermione as an act of vengeance against Menelaus, who has condemned Orestes to death for his matricide. And in *Iphigenia in Tauris,* Pylades accompanies Orestes to the remote shores of the barbaric Taurians, where he has been ordered by an ambiguous oracle to rescue the image of the goddess Artemis (her statue as well as her priestess, Iphigenia). In both plays his steadfast friendship supports an Orestes still rendered vacillating by madness.

2. There is a certain variation among editions; in doubtful cases, and for all line references, I rely on *Aeschyli septem quae supersunt tragoediae,* ed. Gilbert Murray (Oxford: Clarendon, 1952).

3. It is of course possible that this motive was introduced already in the lost lines of the prologue.

4. Here my emphasis differs from that of many scholars—e.g., John Herington,

Aeschylus (New Haven: Yale University Press, 1986), 125, who speaks of Apollo's "stringent orders" to Orestes. I regard his words, rather, as advice: If you don't do this, then that will be the inevitable result.

5. Richard Kuhns, *The House, the City, and the Judge. The Growth of Moral Awareness in the Oresteia* (Indianapolis: Bobbs-Merrill, 1962), 31–33, makes a persuasive case for the moral confusion stemming from Orestes' status as outsider.

6. See, especially, Herbert Jennings Rose, "Aeschylus the Psychologist," *Symbolae Osloenses* 32 (1956): 1–22, which I know only from the German translation: "Aischylos als Psychologe," in *Wege zu Aischylos,* ed. Hildebrecht Hommel, 2 vols. (Darmstadt: Wissenschaftliche Buchgesellschaft, 1974), 1:148–74; Kuhns, *The House, the City, and the Judge,* 8 and 6n1, which takes Orestes' moral growth as its thesis; and Hermann Josef Dirksen, *Die aischyleische Gestalt des Orest und ihre Bedeutung für die Interpretation der Eumeniden* (Nuremberg: Hans Carl, 1965), 111–14. All these works emphasize Orestes' development in the course of *The Libation Bearers,* a view that I find more plausible than that of Thomas G. Rosenmeyer, *The Art of Aeschylus* (Berkeley: University of California Press, 1982), who sees only vacillation (250–51) but no development, and denies the role of motivation and choice in Orestes' behavior (306).

7. Simon Goldhill, *Aeschylus: The Oresteia* (Cambridge: Cambridge University Press, 1992), 41.

8. T. G. Tucker, *Choephori* (Cambridge: Cambridge University Press, 1901), xxxvii–xl, provides a detailed analysis of the incantation.

9. Some commentators—notably George Thomson, *Aeschylus and Athens: A Study in the Social Origins of Drama* (1940; rpt. New York: Haskell House, 1967), 268–69—read the dialectic of the *kommos* differently and see the chorus as retreating from their lust for vengeance as Electra and Orestes increase their fury.

10. Some editors, including George Thomson in *The Oresteia of Aeschylus* (Cambridge: Cambridge University Press, 1938), attribute this speech to Electra; but along with Murray and Tucker, 157, I see no reason to introduce Electra into this scene. The speech obviously casts Clytemnestra in a more favorable light by exposing, at least momentarily, her maternal instincts.

11. Dirksen, *Die aischyleische Gestalt,* 113: "Wendepunkt."

12. Bruno Snell, *Aischylos und das Handeln im Drama, Philologus,* supplemental volume 20/1 (Leipzig, 1928), 126.

13. Snell, *Aischylos und das Handeln im Drama,* 131.

14. See Theodore Ziolkowski, *The Mirror of Justice: Literary Reflections of Legal Crises* (Princeton: Princeton University Press, 1997), 21–30.

15. Tucker, *Choephori,* xxxii.

16. William Arrowsmith, "The Criticism of Greek Tragedy," *Tulane Drama Review* 3 (1959): 31–57; here 48–49.

17. Thomson, *Aeschylus and Athens,* 278–79.

18. Rose, "Aischylos als Psychologe," 153.

19. Dirksen, *Die aischyleische Gestalt des Orest,* 111.

20. Kuhns, *The House, the City, and the Judge,* 8.

21. In *Mirror of Justice,* 31–41, I discuss the legal and theological aspects of *The Eumenides.*

22. Ziolkowski, *Mirror of Justice,* 20, for full references.

23. Arrowsmith, "Criticism of Greek Tragedy," 31–57; here 49. Rosenmeyer, *Art*

of Aeschylus, 304, plays down the moment of hesitation, seeing in it no more than "a delay occasioned by considerations of decorum."

24. Kuhns, *The House, the City, and the Judge,* 29 and 8–9; Dirksen, *Die aischyleische Gestalt des Orest,* 114–16; and Rosenmeyer, *Art of Aeschylus,* 369–76, who, while taking a judiciously restrained view of the links between Aeschylus's dramas and the times in which he lived, notes the "broad spectrum of shared experience" of citizens in Athens.

25. Herington, *Aeschylus,* 15.

26. See Theodore Ziolkowski, *The Sin of Knowledge: Ancient Themes and Modern Variations* (Princeton: Princeton University Press, 2000), 32–42.

27. Dirksen, *Die aischyleische Gestalt des Orest,* 116.

3. Parzival

1. See my essay, "Wagner's *Parsifal* between Mystery and Mummery; or, Race, Class, and Gender in Bayreuth," in *The Return of Thematic Criticism,* ed. Werner Sollors (Cambridge: Harvard University Press, 1993), 261–86.

2. E.g., Bodo Mergell, *Wolfram von Eschenbach und seine französischen Quellen,* 2 vols. (Münster: Aschendorff, 1936–1943).

3. Jessie L. Weston, *From Ritual to Romance* (1919; rpt. Garden City: Anchor, 1957); Konrad Burdach, *Der Gral. Forschungen über seinen Ursprung und seinen Zusammenhang mit der Longinuslegende* (1938; rpt. Darmstadt: Wissenschaftliche Buchgesellschaft, 1974); and Bodo Mergell, *Der Gral in Wolframs Parzival. Entstehung und Ausbildung der Gralsage im Hochmittelalter* (Halle: Niemeyer, 1952).

4. Hermann J. Weigand, "Die epischen Zeitverhältnisse in den Graldichtungen Crestiens und Wolframs," *PMLA* 53 (1938): 917–50; trans. "Narrative Time in the Grail Poems of Chrétien de Troyes and Wolfram von Eschenbach," in H. J. Weigand, *Wolfram's Parzival: Five Essays with an Introduction,* ed. Ursula Hoffmann (Ithaca: Cornell University Press, 1969), 18–74; and Arthur Groos, "Time Reference and the Liturgical Calendar in Wolfram von Eschenbach's *Parzival,*" *Deutsche Vierteljahresschrift für Literaturwissenschaft und Geistesgeschichte* 49 (1975): 43–65; rpt. in his *Romancing the Grail: Genre, Science, and Quest in Wolfram's Parzival* (Ithaca: Cornell University Press, 1995), 119–43.

5. Hermann J. Weigand, "Wolfram's Grail and the Neutral Angels: A Discussion and a Dialogue," *Germanic Review* 29 (1954): 83–95; rpt. in *Wolfram's Parzival,* 120–41.

6. For bibliographical details see the various editions of Joachim Bumke, *Wolfram von Eschenbach* down to the most recent 7th edition (Stuttgart: Metzler, 1997). I refer in the following notes to the 6th edition of 1991.

7. I refer throughout to the Middle High German text as reproduced in the first three volumes of Albert Leitzmann's edition, 5th ed. (Halle: Niemeyer, 1948). The text, divided since Lachmann's early and now standard edition into sixteen books, is conventionally identified by section and line (827 sections of thirty verses each). I have consulted without adopting the readable and reliable English prose translation by A. T. Hatto (New York: Penguin, 1980).

8. On the *Dümmling* theme see David Blamires, *Characterization and Individuality in Wolfram's "Parzival"* (Cambridge: Cambridge University Press, 1966), 105–217, and esp. 142–52.

9. Hermann J. Weigand, "A Jester at the Grail Castle in Wolfram's *Parzival?*" *PMLA* 67 (1952): 485–510; rpt. in his *Wolfram's Parzival,* 75–119.

10. Christa-Maria Kordt, *Parzival in Munsalvaesche. Kommentar zu Buch V/1 von Wolframs Parzival (224,1–248,30)* (Herne: Verlag für Wissenschaft und Kunst, 1997), 149–50, for a thorough recapitulation and bibliography.

11. Bumke, *Wolfram von Eschenbach,* 104–14.

12. On the enormously popular legend of Prester John, see Vlesvolod Slessarev, *Prester John: The Letter and the Legend* (Minneapolis: University of Minnesota Press, 1959).

13. For an extensive and thorough discussion of Parzival's character and its development see Blamires, *Characterization and Individuality,* 105–217 and 301–61. See also Benedikt Mockenhaupt, *Die Frömmigkeit im "Parzival" Wolframs von Eschenbach. Ein Beitrag zur Geschichte des religiösen Geistes in der Lebenswelt des deutschen Mittelalters* (1942; rpt. Darmstadt: Wissenschaftliche Buchgesellschaft, 1968), 77.

14. On the difficult term "zwîvel" see Blamires, *Characterization and Individuality,* 188–208; and Walter Johannes Schröder, *Der Ritter zwischen Welt und Gott. Idee und Problem des Parzivalromans Wolframs von Eschenbach* (Weimar: Böhlau, 1952), 226–30 and 234–42.

15. Mockenhaupt, *Die Frömmigkeit im "Parzival,"* 25–32.

16. Weigand, *Wolfram's Parzival,* 15, suggests that Anfortas and the company of the Grail are also not yet ripe for redemption—a thought, however, that we cannot pursue here given our specific focus on the hero and his hesitation.

17. Blamires, *Characterization and Individuality,* 189 and *passim,* is especially thorough on repeated encounters that reveal stages in Parzival's development.

18. Bumke, *Wolfram von Eschenbach,* 135–39.

19. Bumke (ibid., 135–36) observes that the negative portrayal of courtly life on Parzival's first visit to Arthur's court is based directly on Chrétien's text. The more appreciative depiction of books 14 and 15 appears to reflect Wolfram's own view.

20. On the relationship between the parallel courts of Arthur and the Grail, see Julius Schwietering, *Die deutsche Dichtung des Mittelalters* (Darmstadt: Hermann Gentner, 1957), 160–82.

21. Bumke, *Wolfram von Eschenbach,* 20–21.

22. This dream is usually treated as prophetic, proclaiming the birth of a great ruler; see Bumke, *Wolfram von Eschenbach,* 58. But given its frightening effect on Herzeloyde it might equally well be read as an anticipation of her death caused by Parzival's heartless departure.

23. For a recent summary and bibliography see Bumke, *Wolfram von Eschenbach,* 128–32 and 178–80. See also Mockenhaupt, *Die Frömmigkeit im "Parzival,"* 17–18.

24. Schröder, *Ritter zwischen Welt und Gott,* 118–26.

4. Hamlet

1. A. C. Bradley, *Shakespearean Tragedy: Lectures on Hamlet, Othello, King Lear, Macbeth,* with a foreword by John Bayley (New York: Penguin, 1991), 133. See also Lee A. Jacobus, *Shakespeare and the Dialectic of Certainty* (New York: St. Martin's, 1992), 90: "Volumes have been written on Hamlet's hesitation, though some critics have pointed out that the earliest viewers did not seem specifically disturbed by his not

acting intently." I cite *Hamlet* from *The Complete Works of Shakespeare,* ed. Hardin Craig (Chicago: Scott, Foresman, 1951), 903–43.

2. See Clifford Leach, "The Hesitation of Pyrrhus," in *The Morality of Art.* Essays Presented to G. Wilson Knight, ed. D. W. Jefferson (London: Routledge, 1969), 41–49; and Robert S. Miola, "Vergil in Shakespeare: From Allusion to Imitation," in *The Classical Heritage: Vergil,* ed. Craig Kallendorf (New York: Garland, 1993), 271–89.

3. A. D. Nuttall, *The Stoic in Love: Selected Essays on Literature and Ideas* (New York: Harvester Wheatsheaf, 1989), 32–33, refers less convincingly to the parallel between the ghost of Hamlet's father and Aeneas's encounter with Anchises in the underworld.

4. Robert S. Miola, "Aeneas and Hamlet," *Comparative and Modern Literature* 8 (1988): 275–90.

5. Louise Schleiner, "Latinized Greek Drama in Shakespeare's Writing of *Hamlet,*" *Shakespeare Quarterly* 41 (1990): 29–48.

6. The comparison is made not only by Shakespeare scholars—e.g., Theodore Spencer, *Shakespeare and the Nature of Man,* Lowell Lectures, 1942, 2d ed. (New York: Macmillan, 1949), 210–11. Classicists also allude almost ritually to the analogy: e.g., T. G. Tucker in his edition of *Choephori* (Cambridge: Cambridge University Press, 1901), lviii, n. 2; or Simon Goldhill, *Aeschylus: The Oresteia* (Cambridge: Cambridge University Press, 1992), 26–27. The most detailed comparison was undertaken by Gilbert Murray in his Annual Shakespeare Lecture for the British Academy: *Hamlet and Orestes: A Study in Traditional Types* (New York: Oxford University Press, 1914), most of which was reprinted in his *Classical Tradition in Poetry* (1927; rpt. New York: Vintage, 1957), 180–210. (Murray's findings are recapitulated by Nuttall, *Stoic in Love,* 34–37.) Many of my points of comparison overlap with Murray's, but, surprisingly, neither he nor Nuttall attributes any significance to the moment of hesitation.

7. W. H. Auden, *The Enchafèd Flood* (1950; rpt. New York: Vintage, 1967), 11. However, it is difficult to agree with his suggestion in the same context that Orestes, in distinction, is already a hero thrust into a tragic situation. Both, after all, are untested young men at the beginning of their respective plays.

8. Bradley, *Shakespearean Tragedy,* 104.

9. Goethe's characterization is in his novel *Wilhelm Meister's Apprenticeship* (*Wilhelm Meisters Lehrjahre,* bk. 4, chap. 13). But see also Bradley, *Shakespearean Tragedy,* 109ff.

10. Spencer, *Shakespeare and the Nature of Man,* 94.

11. Roland M. Frye, *The Renaissance Hamlet: Issues and Responses in 1600* (Princeton: Princeton University Press, 1984), 171–77.

12. Harry Levin, *The Question of Hamlet* (New York: Oxford University Press, 1959), 74.

13. Stephen Greenblatt, *Hamlet in Purgatory* (Princeton: Princeton University Press, 2001), points out that the state-sanctioned church of Shakespeare's time condemned the idea of purgatory as a fiction, but that within the play Hamlet accepts its reality. I would sharpen the thought a bit: Hamlet tries hard to persuade his rational mind that purgatory exists.

14. Spencer, *Shakespeare and the Nature of Man,* 108.

15. See Theodore Ziolkowski, "The Novel of the Thirty-Year-Old," in *Dimensions of the Modern Novel: German Texts and European Contexts* (Princeton: Princeton Uni-

versity Press, 1969), 258–88. While I do not discuss Hamlet, he perfectly fits the model adumbrated there.

16. Bernard McElroy, *Shakespeare's Mature Tragedies* (Princeton: Princeton University Press, 1973), 54 and 3.

17. Maynard Mack, "The Readiness Is All," in *Everybody's Shakespeare: Reflections Chiefly on the Tragedies* (Lincoln: University of Nebraska Press, 1993), 107–27; here 109. Mack's chapter is a lightly revised version of his article "The World of Hamlet," *Yale Review* 41 (1952): 502–24. Note also the evocative title of Levin's *Question of Hamlet*. Levin observes that the key word "question" occurs no fewer than seventeen times in the course of the play (33–34).

18. Levin, *Question of Hamlet*, 49.

19. Frye, *Renaissance Hamlet*, 14–24, on contemporary attitudes toward ghosts.

20. Ibid., 82–102, on contemporary practices regarding deaths and weddings.

21. Various critics have felt that Hamlet's delay is "unmotivated" and that the question about it is "misconceived and misleading." See, for example, Hardin Craig's introductory comments in *The Complete Works of Shakespeare*, 902; and Ruth Nevo, *Tragic Form in Shakespeare* (Princeton: Princeton University Press, 1972), 129.

22. G. W. F. Hegel, *Ästhetik*, ed. Friedrich Bassenge, 2d ed., 2 vols. (Frankfurt am Main: Europäische Verlagsanstalt, 1966), 1:228–29.

23. Edward Engelberg, *The Unknown Distance: From Consciousness to Conscience* (Cambridge: Harvard University Press, 1972), 8–39, esp. 14–15. See also Bradley, *Shakespearean Tragedy*, 100–103; and Frye, *Renaissance Hamlet*, 177–83.

24. Richard A. Posner, *Law and Literature*, rev. ed. (Cambridge: Harvard University Press, 1998), 75–85, also believes that Hamlet "spares Claudius for a bad reason" (81). But in his single-minded reading of the play as a revenge drama he sees Hamlet merely as "a bungler at revenge" and ignores the larger intellectual and philosophical issues at play in the work.

25. Caroline Spurgeon, *Shakespeare's Imagery* (1935; rpt. Cambridge: Cambridge University Press, 1936), is the classic study. She catalogs disease images in *Hamlet* (316–18), esp. "ulcer or tumour, as descriptive of the unwholesome condition morally."

26. Georg Lukács, *The Historical Novel*, trans. Hannah and Stanley Mitchell (Boston: Beacon, 1963), 144.

27. Mack, "The Readiness Is All," 120.

28. McElroy, *Shakespeare's Mature Tragedies*, 34.

29. Murray, *Classical Tradition*, 200.

30. Jessie L. Weston, *From Ritual to Romance* (1919; rpt. Garden City: Anchor, 1957).

31. Nevo, *Tragic Form*, 165. But see also generally Levin, *Question of Hamlet*, and Spencer, *Shakespeare and the Nature of Man*.

32. E.g., Spencer, *Shakespeare and the Nature of Man*, 21–50; but see also Levin, *Question of Hamlet*, 72–75; and many subsequent studies.

33. *The Complete Poetry of John Donne*, ed. John T. Shawcross (Garden City: Anchor, 1967), 270–86.

34. See Greenblatt, *Hamlet in Purgatory*.

35. McElroy, *Shakespeare's Mature Tragedies*, 34.

36. The following paragraphs recapitulate several pages of Theodore Ziolkowski,

The Mirror of Justice: Literary Reflections of Legal Crises (Princeton: Princeton University Press, 1997), 167–74.

37. I cite the text according to the pagination of the authorized edition (London, 1635) as reproduced in *Archeion,* ed. Charles H. McIlwain and Paul L. Ward (Cambridge: Harvard University Press, 1957).

38. Mark Edwin Andrews, *Law versus Equity in "The Merchant of Venice"* (Boulder: University of Colorado Press, 1965), xi.

39. I take anomy to be something quite different from the tragedy of reflection, as understood by Romantic critics, which is reasonably rejected by Bradley, *Shakespearean Tragedy,* 106–8.

40. Spencer, *Shakespeare and the Nature of Man,* 106, makes the point that even the "grammatical chaos of his utterances" marks Hamlet's emotional turmoil in his first soliloquy.

5. *Wallenstein*

1. Humboldt to Schiller, early September 1800; Humboldt's lengthy essay-letter on *Wallenstein* is reprinted in *Schillers Werke,* Nationalausgabe, vol. 38, pt. 1 (Weimar: Böhlau, 1975), 322–39; here 323.

2. Anne Louise Germaine de Staël, *De l'Allemagne,* ed. André Monchoux (Paris: Didier, 1956), 168.

3. In Thomas Carlyle, *Life of Friedrich Schiller* (New York: Alden, 1885), 150.

4. Thomas Mann, "Versuch über Schiller," in *Gesammelte Werke in zwölf Bänden* (Oldenburg: Fischer, 1960), 9:911: "europäische Optik, universelle Übersicht."

5. See the reviews and essays reprinted in *Schillers Wallenstein,* ed. Fritz Heuer and Werner Keller (Darmstadt: Wissenschaftliche Buchgesellschaft, 1977); and Helmut G. Hermann's bibliography attached to Walter Hinderer's review-essay *Der Mensch in der Geschichte: Ein Versuch über Schillers Wallenstein* (Königstein: Athenäum, 1980), 99–138.

6. Stephen Spender, "Schiller, Shakespeare and the Theme of Power," in *A Schiller Symposium. In Observance of the Bicentenary of Schiller's Birth,* ed. A. Leslie Willson (University of Texas, Austin: Department of Germanic Languages, 1960), 49–61; here 60.

7. Gisela N. Berns, *Greek Antiquity in Schiller's Wallenstein* (Chapel Hill: University of North Carolina Press, 1985), 76.

8. Hinderer, *Mensch in der Geschichte,* 2; and Peter-André Alt, *Schiller: Leben—Werk—Zeit,* vol. 2 (Munich: Beck, 2000), 420–64.

9. On the plans for the edition see the letters excerpted in *Dichter über ihre Dichtungen: Friedrich Schiller (Von den Anfängen bis 1795),* ed. Bodo Lecke (Munich: Heimeran, 1969), 649–54; the quotation, 658, is from Schiller's letter to Charlotte von Lengefeld and Karoline von Beulwitz, 4 Dec. 1788; *Schillers Briefe,* ed. Fritz Jonas, 7 vols. (Stuttgart: Deutsche Verlagsanstalt, 1892–96), 2:170.

10. Schiller's letter to Goethe of 22 February 1795, for instance, suggests his response to the novel's *Hamlet* sections; *Schillers Briefe,* 4:133.

11. George Steiner, *The Death of Tragedy* (New York: Knopf, 1961), 158.

12. Alt, *Schiller,* 2:437.

13. I follow the text as printed in *Sämtliche Werke*, ed. Gerhard Fricke and Herbert G. Göpfert, 4th ed., 5 vols. (Munich: Hanser, 1965), 2:269–547.

14. Steiner, *Death of Tragedy*, 181.

15. There is a vast bibliography on the subject. A reliable, readable introduction is provided by C. V. Wedgwood, *The Thirty Years' War* (London: Cape, 1938).

16. Schiller to Körner, 28 Nov. 1791; *Schillers Briefe*, 3:170.

17. For our purposes it is unnecessary to recapitulate the exhaustively treated questions concerning the stages of composition, the relationship of the play to Schiller's *History* and to his theory of tragedy, the true nature of Wallenstein's vision of a unified Germany, or the character of his melancholy.

18. Historians and biographers have been fiercely divided regarding the fascinating and ambiguous character of Wallenstein, ranging from denunciations for his treachery and megalomania to eulogies for his far-reaching idealism. See Golo Mann, *Wallenstein: His Life Narrated*, trans. Charles Kessler (New York: Holt, Rinehart, Winston, 1976).

19. Carlyle, *Life of Schiller*, 130.

20. Ibid., 129.

21. Staël, *De l'Allemagne*, 169.

22. Carlyle, *Life of Schiller*, 142.

23. Staël, *De l'Allemagne*, 170.

24. Clemens Heselhaus, "Wallensteins Welttheater," *Der Deutschunterricht* 12 (1960): 42–71, discusses Wallenstein's tactics as an aesthetic reluctance to contaminate his ideas with the reality of the world. Oskar Seidlin, "Wallenstein: Sein und Zeit," in *Von Goethe zu Thomas Mann* (Göttingen: Vandenhoeck & Ruprecht, 1963), 120–35, presents the retarding delays as an attempt to freeze time aesthetically into the new era that he longs to create. Both essays are reprinted in Heuer/Keller, *Schillers Wallenstein*, 213–36, 237–53.

25. Max Kommerell, "Schiller als Psychologe," in *Geist und Buchstabe der Dichtung*, 4th ed. (Frankfurt am Main: Klostermann, 1956), 214: "Überweiber."

26. Hermann J. Weigand, "Schiller: Transfiguration of a Titan," in *Surveys and Soundings in European Literature*, ed. A. Leslie Willson (Princeton: Princeton University Press, 1966), 73–123; here 117–18.

27. Staël, *De l'Allemagne*, 173.

28. G. W. F. Hegel, "Über Wallenstein," in *Werke in 20 Bänden*, ed. Eva Moldenhauer and Karl Markus Michel (Frankfurt am Main: Suhrkamp, 1986), 1: 618–20; rpt. Heuer/Keller, *Schillers Wallenstein*, 15–16.

29. Dieter Borchmeyer, *Macht und Melancholie. Schillers Wallenstein* (Frankfurt am Main: Athenäum, 1988); and Leslie Sharpe, *Schiller: Drama, Thought, and Politics* (Cambridge: Cambridge University Press, 1991), 227–34.

30. Søren Kierkegaard, *Either/Or*, vol. 2, trans. Walter Lowrie, rev. Howard A. Johnson (Princeton: Princeton University Press, 1971), 171.

31. George A. Wells, "Astrology in Schiller's *Wallenstein*," *Journal of English and Germanic Philology* 68 (1969): 100–115; here 103n4, citing with approval the argument to this effect in R. Marleyn, "*Wallenstein* and the Structure of Schiller's Tragedies," *Germanic Review* 32 (1957): 186–99.

32. Max Kommerell, "Schiller als Gestalter des handelnden Menschen," in *Geist und Buchstabe*, 132–74; here 147. Borchmeyer, *Macht und Melancholie*, 74–77, com-

pares Wallenstein and Hamlet with regard to their melancholy but with no analysis of the reasons for, and results of, their hesitations and delays.

33. Schiller, *Sämtliche Werke*, 4:430, and 4:423: "die böhmischen Rebellen."

34. See, for instance, Sharpe, *Friedrich Schiller*, 217–50; esp. 217–18, 248–50.

35. Kommerell, "Schiller als Psychologe," 189.

36. Spender, "Schiller, Shakespeare and the Theme of Power," 58–59.

37. Weigand, "Schiller: Transfiguration of a Titan," 118.

6. Wavering Heroes

1. Edgar Quinet, *Merlin l'Enchanteur* (Paris: Michel Lévy, 1860), 1: x: "trop faible, . . . trop corrompu, trop usé; . . . l'haleine lui manque pour parcourir des horizons étendus."

2. G. W. F. Hegel, *Ästhetik*, ed. Friedrich Bassenge, 2d ed., 2 vols. (Frankfurt am Main: Europäische Verlagsanstalt, 1966), 1:185–86.

3. I cite the text of the first edition as provided in the admirable edition: *Waverley; or, 'Tis Sixty Years Since*, ed. Claire Lamont (Oxford: Clarendon, 1981).

4. Quoted in Richard Humphrey, *Walter Scott: Waverley* (Cambridge: Cambridge University Press, 1993), 50.

5. Alexander Welsh, *The Hero of the Waverley Novels* (New Haven: Yale University Press, 1963), 30–57; here 35. Welsh's book, with three new essays, was reissued in 1992 by Princeton University Press.

6. Georg Lukács, *The Historical Novel* (1937), trans. Hannah and Stanley Mitchell (Boston: Beacon, 1963), 37.

7. Mario Praz, *The Hero in Eclipse in Victorian Fiction*, trans. Angus Davidson (London: Oxford University Press, 1956), 224–25.

8. Johann Peter Eckermann, *Gespräche mit Goethe*, ed. H. H. Houben, 9th ed. (Leipzig: Brockhause, 1909), 230 (9 October 1828).

9. David Daiches, *Sir Walter Scott and His World* (London: Thames and Hudson, 1971), 97.

10. In the fifteenth of *Paul's Letters to His Kinsfolk*, 3d ed. (Edinburgh: Constable, 1816), 432–33.

11. Scott's oppositions and polarities have been often noted. Humphrey, *Walter Scott*, provides perhaps the finest analysis of the historical context of Scott's novel. But see also Daiches, *Sir Walter Scott*; and Lukács, *Historical Novel*, 30–63.

12. Humphrey, *Walter Scott*, 2–3, cites the opinions of various historians.

13. Ibid., 42.

14. Lars Hartveit, *Dream within a Dream: A Thematic Approach to Scott's Vision of Fictional Reality* (New York: Humanities Press, 1974), 72–118 ("The Heroic: *Waverley*"). On the "trance-like," even "visionary" state of Scott's heroes see also Virgil Nemoianu, *The Taming of Romanticism: European Literature and the Age of Biedermeier* (Cambridge: Harvard University Press, 1984), 62–69.

15. Hartveit, *Dream within a Dream*, 74.

16. Lukács, *Historical Novel*, 33–34.

17. Lukács (*ibid.*, 39–40) notes the parallel to Hegel's philosophy of history, but restricts his analysis to Fergus Mac-Ivor as a Hegelian "world-historical individual"

who represents "the reactionary side of Stuart Restoration attempts." Lukács does not go on to discuss the overall progress of the novel in Hegelian terms.

18. G. W. F. Hegel, *Vorlesungen über die Philosophie der Geschichte,* ed. Eva Moldenhauer and Karl Markus Michel, vol. 12 of *Werke in 20 Bänden* (Frankfurt am Main: Suhrkamp, 1986), 11–141; esp. 133–41.

19. Lukács, *Historical Novel,* 53. On *Waverley* as a historical novel, see also Fabian Lampart, *Zeit und Geschichte: Die mehrfachen Anfänge des historischen Romans bei Scott, Arnim, Vigny und Manzoni* (Würzburg: Königshausen & Neumann, 2002), 77–166.

20. Lukács, *Historical Novel,* 19–30; Daiches, *Sir Walter Scott and His World,* 58–62; and Humphrey, *Walter Scott: Waverley,* 14–21, give good, brief accounts of these changes.

21. Hegel, *Ästhetik,* 1:180–92.

22. Friedrich Dürrenmatt, "Theaterprobleme," in *Werkausgabe in dreißig Bänden* (Zurich: Diogenes, 1985), 24:31–72; here 60.

23. Thomas Carlyle, *Heroes, Hero-Worship and the Heroic in History* (New York: Alden, 1885), 185–230; here 185.

24. Sean O'Faolain, *The Vanishing Hero: Studies in Novelists of the Twenties* (London: Eyre & Spottiswoode, 1956); and Mario Praz, *Hero in Eclipse.*

25. Raymond Giraud, *The Unheroic Hero in the Novels of Stendhal, Balzac, and Flaubert* (New Brunswick: Rutgers University Press, 1957); Allan H. Pasco, *Sick Heroes: French Society and Literature in the Romantic Age, 1750–1850* (Exeter: University of Exeter Press, 1997).

26. Pasco, *Sick Heroes,* 6–7.

27. Ibid., 11–15.

28. Nor Giraud's "unheroic heroes," (185–88), who are restricted by being defined essentially in opposition to "the classic Cornelian type of hero."

29. Mikhail Yurevich Lermontov, *A Hero of Our Own Times,* trans. Eden and Cedar Paul (London: Oxford University Press, 1958).

30. Fyodor Dostoyevsky, *Notes from Underground and The Double,* trans. Jessie Coulson (Harmondsworth: Penguin, 1972).

31. See Victor Brombert's essay "Dostoevsky's Underground Man: Portrait of the Paradoxalist," in *In Praise of Antiheroes: Figures and Themes in Modern European Literature, 1830–1980* (Chicago: University of Chicago Press, 1999), 31–42.

32. Miguel de Unamuno, *Mist: A Tragicomic Novel,* trans. Warner Fite, foreword by Theodore Ziolkowski (Urbana: University of Illinois Press, 2000).

33. Miguel de Unamuno, *Our Lord Don Quixote: The Life of Don Quixote and Sancho with Related Essays,* trans. Anthony Kerrigan, Bollingen Series 85, 3 (Princeton: Princeton University Press, 1967), 323.

34. See Theodore Ziolkowski, "Figures on Loan: The Boundaries of Literature and Life," in *Varieties of Literary Thematics* (Princeton: Princeton University Press, 1983), 123–51.

35. Theodore Ziolkowski, "Franz Kafka: *The Trial,*" in *Dimensions of the Modern Novel: German Texts and European Contexts* (Princeton: Princeton University Press, 1969), 37–67.

36. "Er," in Franz Kafka, *Beschreibung eines Kampfs. Novellen, Skizzen und Aphorismen aus dem Nachlass* (New York: Schocken, 1946), 283.

37. "Observations on Sin, Suffering, Hope, and the True Way," in *Hochzeitsvor-*

bereitungen auf dem Lande und andere Prosa aus dem Nachlass, ed. Max Brod (Frankfurt am Main: Fischer, 1966), 49–50.

38. Frank Kafka, *The Trial,* trans. Will and Edwin Muir, rev. by E. M. Butler (New York: Modern Library, 1956), 285.

39. Raymond Williams, in *Modern Tragedy* (1966; rev. ed., London: Verso, 1979), offers a similar reading of modern (post-Hegelian) dramatic tragedy, which by his account ends when the hero reaches one of several conditions: victimhood, a tragic deadlock, private or social tragedy, resignation or despair; otherwise the author, like Brecht, simply rejects tragedy altogether. To reach this definition of "modern" tragedy, of course, Williams must broaden his understanding of the "hero" well beyond the conventional concept.

Conclusion: Continuities

1. Included as an appendix in *A Contribution to the Critique of Political Economy,* trans. N. I. Stone (Chicago: Kerr, 1904), 311. I have slightly modified the translation.

2. E.g., Raymond Williams, *Modern Tragedy* (1966; rev. ed., London: Verso, 1979), 13–15 and 46–54, who discusses the distinction while arguing for a looser, more inclusive usage.

3. I write this sentence in the week when *Time* magazine is featuring as its "Persons of the Year 2002" three women nominated for their courage as whistle-blowers in their various male-dominated organizations.

Index

Parry, Adam, 12
Parzival, 2–5, 141, 143; and Orestes, 64
Pasco, Allan H., 132
Pavlov, I. P., 23
Peisistratus, 50
Pericles, 50
Philipp of Swabia, 72
Piccolomini, Octavio, 99
Pius V, pope, 91
Possevino, Antonio, 14
Praz, Mario, 121, 131

Quinet, Edgar, *Merlin,* 120
Quinn, Kenneth, 16

Robinson, Henry Crabb, 121

St. German, Christopher, *Doctor and Student,* 93
Sallust, 27–28, 31
Saxo Grammaticus, 88
Schiller, Friedrich, 4, 97–98, 142; *On Aesthetic Education,* 117; and his age, 115–18; *History of Thirty Years' War,* 100, 115–16; and *Hamlet,* 114–15; *Piccolominis,* 102–8; "Prolog," 11, 102, 115; and Shakespeare, 97–98; *Wallenstein,* 98–100; *Wallenstein's Camp,* 101–02; *Wallenstein's Death,* 108–13; and *Waverley,* 121–23, 126–27. *See also* Wallenstein
Scott, Sir Walter, 134, 139; and English history, 128–30, 142; and Hegel, 127; *Wallenstein,* 121–23, 126–27; *Waverley,* 5–6, 120–27
Servius, 17, 26
Shakespeare, William, and his age, 4, 88–95, 142; *Hamlet,* 74–75, 77–88
Sherrington, C. S., 23
Smith, Roger, 3

Sophocles, *Electra,* 34–35, 43
Spender, Stephen, 97, 117
Spengler, Oswald, 50
Staël, Germaine de, 96–97, 102, 106, 113–14
Steiner, George, 98
Strauss, Richard, *Ekektra,* 43
Suerbaum, Werner, 17
Sulla, 26–27, 31
Syme, Ronald, 31

Tacitus, 31
Tasso, Torquato, *Gerusalemme liberata,* 14–15
Thirty Years' War, 98–100, 116
Thomas, Richard F., 16
Toynbee, Arnold, 32
"Trojan Dilemma," 51–52, 140–41

Unamuno, Miguel de, 136–37; *Mist,* 6, 135–36, 142–43

Vegius, Mapheus, 13–14
Virgil, and his age, 26–29; and Augustus, 29–31; *Aeneid,* 9–11, 17–22; as bildungsroman, 33; as comment on the age, 4, 28–33, 141; and differing views of ending, 12–17

Wagner, Richard, *Parsifal,* 54–56
Wallenstein, 2–5, 141–43; and Hamlet, 114–15; and Waverley, 121–23, 126–27
Wallenstein, Albrecht von, 99
Weber, Max, 8
Wolfram von Eschenbach, 4, 70; and his age, 70–72, 142; *Parzival,* 55–67; *Parzival* as cultural criticism, 67–70. *See also* Parzival

ABOUT THE AUTHOR

THEODORE ZIOLKOWSKI is Class of 1900 Professor Emeritus of German and Comparative Literature at Princeton University. He is the author of many books, including *Virgil and the Moderns*, *The Mirror of Justice* (which received Phi Beta Kappa's Christian Gauss Award), and *The Sin of Knowledge: Ancient Themes and Modern Variations*.